DUMBBELLS TO DIAMONDS

33 WORKOUTS TO MEGA WEALTH

BOB CHEEK

Hardie Grant

BOOKS

Published in 2022 by Hardie Grant Books an imprint of Hardie Grant Publishing

Hardie Grant Books (Melbourne)
Ground Floor, Building 1, 658 Church Street
Richmond VIC 3121, Australia

Hardie Grant Books (London)
5th and 6th Floors,52–54 Southwark Street
London SE1 1UN, United Kingdom

www.hardiegrant.com.au

Hardie Grant acknowledges the Traditional Owners of the country on which we work, the Wurundjeri people of the Kulin nation and the Gadigal people of the Eora nation, and recognises their continuing connection to the land, waters and culture. We pay our respects to their Elders past and present.

While the publisher has made every effort to obtain all relevant copyright licences, any parties with further information or claim to copyright are invited to contact the publisher directly.

A catalogue record of this book is available from the National Library of Australia.

Dumbbells to Diamonds: 33 workouts to mega wealth

ISBN 9781743798560

Edited by Sally Moss
Cover illustration by John Farmer
Printed in Australia by Ovato

For my talented grandchildren, Nellie, Olivia, Molly, William, Otis and Betty, in the hope that it inspires you to never give up on pursuing your dreams.

CONTENTS

THE
PREPARATION

first contemplated writing a book about the insane gym industry, which I'd just departed, while lounging on the rooftop sundeck of my Melbourne townhouse. I'd just sold my business for more than $50 million – eight years after I'd started it from little more than an idea and plenty of hope.

I still couldn't believe my good fortune. Satisfaction and a certain smugness filled my senses as I gazed at the massive Jewish fortresses across the street: expensive, indestructible edifices reflecting lives of frugality, discipline and savvy investing.

Talk about hit or miss. And luck. Hell, when this naive Tasmanian decided to enter the ultra-competitive Melbourne gym market, he didn't even know that Caulfield North and the surrounding heartland, where he set up headquarters, was the epicentre of Victorian Jewry. Although the bagels and kosher butcher shops should've been a clue.

The Jews get on with their lives and value privacy. The curt nod of the head in the street instead of the "how 'ya going mate" greeting in Tassie, where everyone knows everyone, was disconcerting at first. But I grew to like it, and the peace and quiet.

Somehow in this environment a book seemed futile, pretentious and self-indulgent, as though I was trying to relive my brief political notoriety. No, better to live in a shroud of privacy, just like my neighbours.

Later came the COVID-19 pandemic. I was in the United States and cut short a trip to return home into self-isolation. With isolation came the urge to write again: what else does a former journo do when housebound and alone?

The fitness industry was in chaos; gyms were being forced to shut, including the chain I'd just sold. When the only aim is survival, it's not a great time to give advice on how to run a fitness business.

But dreams never die. I had opened our first Zap during the global financial crisis, when everyone was certain the world of capitalism had collapsed forever. And I did it in Tasmania, the Jurassic Park of Australia at that time (but no longer), where most visitors thought the world had already ended.

And yet out of misfortune sprang plenty of opportunity: rents were cheap and government stimulus abounded. The same will happen for the brave and persistent from the depths of COVID-19.

After all, running gyms – and most businesses – is 80 per cent commonsense. Unfortunately most people lack that basic commodity.

I've been in the gym industry – on and off – for a long time. So it was also important to take people on the same rollicking four decade time-machine ride through the world of workouts that I'd experienced firsthand; from the unwanted, ridiculed, despised dens of rip-offs and con men in the 1980s to the new twenty-first century fantasyland of aspiration, image, wellbeing and the pursuit of eternal youth. From the grunts and groans of nineteenth-century circus strongmen to Arnold Schwarzenegger pumping iron at Venice Beach and the shock of Jane Fonda leading, or should I say leotarding, a new female invasion of a then male-dominated industry, gyms have become the temples of modern strength and perfection. A brand-new religion for millions of narcissistic, Instagram-snapping devotees, seeking solace from the realities of life in an oasis of cardio machines, high-intensity workouts, weight plates and, most importantly, mirrors.

And gyms, with their new-found respectability as trendy spaces, have lured fortune-seeking venture capitalists, entrepreneurs, celebrities, personal trainers and just everyday fitness fanatics – like miners to the promise of gold. But, as the history of gold mining has shown, most have walked away with empty pockets and broken dreams.

This book is my gym story: the tale of how a bloke approaching sixty-five years of age – washed up and broken after an ill-fated foray into politics – turned one loss-making gym into a fitness empire and sold out just eight years later for more than $50 million. It took me nearly forty years to learn how to make money from gyms; others haven't been so fortunate. The industry spits out bankrupt owners like a set of clean-and-jerks (and there are plenty of jerks). They soon learn that, despite the laudable vision of helping others, gyms are also a business. Sadly, most budding entrepreneurs are unprepared and many buckle under the weight of bottom-line expectations and the stress of handling staff, members and bankers.

My dream, to develop a gym chain known as Zap Fitness 24/7, turned on its head an outdated fitness industry hamstrung by archaic rules. In the process Zap enjoyed the biggest profit margins of any health and wellness operation in Australia. All without borrowing any money and owning nothing more than an incredible brand; everything else was hired, leased or rented. I ended up with a chain of thirty-seven gyms covering three Australian states. Not one was franchised, as most are today. They were all lovingly developed by my company – treadmill by treadmill, dumbbell by dumbbell, rubber tile by rubber tile, setback by setback, triumph by triumph.

Greece (800BC): The moment exercising in the nude became less popular...

THE WARM-UP

Gyms began about 2,800 years ago in ancient Greece, and many times during my career in the industry I felt at least that old. Other days, while helping people lead healthier, happier, more productive lives and still managing to make a quid, I thought I'd discovered the fountain – or should I say protein shake – of youth.

It's that sort of industry: love it one day, hate it the next.

The Greek word *gymnasion*, from which the name gymnasium derives, means working out in the nude; which, apparently, the Greeks eagerly embraced in the warm Mediterranean sun. I'm not sure it would have proved as popular in the depths of a Tasmanian winter, although it's amazing how the eagerness to show off a buffed new body overcomes any temporary hardships.

Like the Greeks, this book exposes the naked truth about the gym game: the dark side and its foibles and traps for the unwary.

Amazingly, the nucleus of the gym business is still much the same as in 800 BC. We do make some attempt to cover our bodies in often-fashionable, over-priced designer workout gear, but we still lift weights for strength, ramp up the heart rate for stamina and worship the body beautiful.

The Greeks even had medicine balls fashioned from skins and handheld weights made of stone or metal – an early version of dumbbells – which they called *halteres*.

Dumbbells are still the staple piece of equipment in any gym: the workhorses. They're cheap and reliable, get results and last forever, unlIke costly treadmills and other electronic and cabled machines. That's why you see racks of them dominating strength-training sections – staid, and usually dressed in black and metal grey, but always gazing contemptuously at the latest fad machines, like the royal family of gymland.

No one is sure where the word dumbbell originated. The first mention was in England in 1711, when the essayist Joseph Addison wrote about exercising with a "dumb bell" in an essay for *The Spectator* magazine.

It's thought that athletes used hand-held church bells to strengthen their upper bodies and arms. But swinging a church bell in the wee hours and waking up all the dogs and villagers didn't prove popular. So they got rid of the clapper (gong part) and peace was restored.

From that time on, they were known as "dumb" bells, as in no sound. When the first strongmen and circus performers began to make their own equipment, with handles, they still kept the name.

Business is just like a gym workout: the harder you toil and sweat, the better the result – provided you have the right exercise regimen. This book will ensure you do. You'll be a "smart" bell, not a "dumb" bell.

To keep the theme, I've called the chapters in this book workouts: your personal training program for making ultra-profits and being successful. How to turn your dumbbells into diamonds.

GET ME OUT OF HERE!

Most people look forward to retirement: the twilight years without any work pressure; golden, sun-filled days of golf, gardening, travel, grandkids and memories. Not me. Memories are nightmares. Panic, anxiety, post-mortems and the dreaded what-ifs. Sure, I'm heading towards sixty-five – an old fart in most people's eyes. But hell, retirement. No, please, no!

My thoughts stutter in unison with the disjointed gyrations of what I still stubbornly call "going for a run". Sadly, the once sprightly jog has become a slow shuffle, knees locked as if dipped in concrete; desperately trying to raise each Nike-clad foot higher than the pavement as I trundle down Hobart's Sandy Bay Road on an early Saturday morning in late spring. My son Marcus – who once played footy, cricket and tennis with his old man – now says running with Dad is like taking the dog for a walk. A dog. Gone forever is the spring of a startled gazelle; welcome arthritic Labrador.

I'm broke: no money. No future. No golden years. Plod. Plod. Plod. Worry. Worry. Worry.

I try to stay positive. Self-talk. Relax and let the go-get-'em green ink flow through the brain as always, creating a cascade of new ideas. The majestic River Derwent surges alongside, pulling me along with the tide as it rushes in from the frozen turbulence of the Southern Ocean.

It's no good. Today's different. My mind is cluttered with red, negative, stop-sign fluid; my brain is acting like a blotter, not a conduit for great invention. A vision of hip replacements and seniors cards, bingo nights, walking frames and nursing homes stretches before my bloodshot eyes, seemingly all the way to the summit of the brooding, distant Mount Wellington... and down the other side into the darkness.

I used to be a politician – a damn good one, I thought. Most people didn't agree. I had a go and stood for something, many things actually. Conviction – there's not much of it left now, with the benches full of career university graduates, trade-union hacks and former political apparatchiks. No life experience there. They all have one aim – to get re-elected – and be damned with what's best for the people.

I was Leader of the Opposition. Leader of the Tasmanian Liberal Party. Leader of a big part of the island's community. Head of everything, really. Pretty shit-hot. I had an ornate, antique-laden office in Hobart's historic Parliament House; dozens of staff; and lifetime superannuation on the horizon, locking in my family's financial security.

Super: those taxpayer-funded rivers of gold that usually flow, like the Derwent, into your bank account when you finally say farewell to politics; or, in my case, politics says goodbye to you.

I lost the election – and my seat. And didn't qualify for super. It still hurts.

The day before the disastrous election I was earning about $300,000 a year and benefitting from plenty of taxpayer-funded perks. The day after, nothing... zilch. Before I stood for parliament, I bragged that I didn't care about super; I was there for the good of the nation and my electorate. Truth is, I wanted and needed it, badly.

Enough about politics (you can read the full story in my book *Cheeky: Confessions of a Ferret Salesman*).

I continue stumbling along the scenic roadway; the early morning mist now blankets the Derwent, matching my mood, smothering the sunlight that normally dances off the water like a thousand sequined ballerinas. I feel as though I'm in a Legoland of heavily mortgaged houses, dappled white-and-grey blocks of Hobart aspiration rising steeply up the convict-cleared hillsides to stare down at this ghostly figurine of misfortune.

Sandy Bay, my home of thirty years, is the blue-ribbon suburb in the electorate of Denison (now called Clark). My wife, Stephanie, and I raised our kids here. In my time in politics I shook every hand in the neighbourhood, knew most residents by their first name. I still love the place, still enjoy the peace and quiet and the slower pace.

On I trudge. The silence is broken by arthritis-racked knees as bone grinds on bone like a starved Rottweiler feasting on roadkill. To drown out the splintering framework, I crank up the volume of my anthem, "Chariots of Fire", on the iPod. I used to play this for inspiration before Question Time in parliament. Don't know about the chariots, but I was fired all right.

More negative thoughts.

Thermos flask-shaped Wrest Point casino looms ahead, the place where I made my tearful concession speech just a few short years ago. I can't escape the past whatever I do.

Grate. Grate. Grate.

Last month a Melbourne orthopaedic surgeon took another agonised look at my knee X-rays, backlit on the wall. Then he winced, shook his head, and blurted, "Buy yourself a bike."

"I can't fit on a bike, I'm all arms and legs," I protested. "Why?"

"Because you can't keep running on tin legs," he hissed. "How many times do I have to tell you? Keep doing it and you'll need knee replacements. Or worse." With that, he turned back to the young intern

in the room and dismissed me. I didn't get time to ask him what "or worse" meant.

Of course, I didn't take his advice and I kept running, like all ageing idiots who think they're invincible. In my Peter Pan world, the commendable silver-haired pursuits of walking, riding, bowls, or whatever, are considered acts of treason: waving the white flag to the invaders of longevity. After all, at fifty-one I had run a marathon just for the hell of it, and to prove I could.

Desperately, pathetically, I try to convince myself that I'm ten years younger and approaching fifty-five. To facilitate the charade, I refuse to accept seniors card discounts; swear at anyone who offers me a seat on a crowded bus or train; banish all mirrors from the house; and pity the poor person who foolishly inquires if I'm eligible for a pensioner rate. "Bob's gone senile," people whisper.

I remember an American motivational speaker at one of the many fitness conventions I've attended: "Get up early," she screamed at her startled audience of young, dewy-eyed personal trainers, "draw back the drapes, look out the window and shout, 'Good morning God!' Then, as if she's going to be sleeping with everyone to make sure we greet God the right way, she adds: "Don't ever let me hear you say, 'God, it's morning'." Well, sorry Sandy (I think that was her name) this is definitely my "God, it's morning" day, whether you like it or not.

Instead of super, I've got a gym that's losing thousands of dollars each year. I can hardly afford to pay the staff, let alone myself. I've owned gyms on and off for the best part of twenty-five years; made a bit, lost a lot. Deep down loved the hype and glamour of the world's most narcissistic, self-centred industry. Suited my vanity, so I was told. Unfortunately, because my latest gym was unsaleable, I kept it while sacrificing my life on the altar of political futility. If parliamentary super is a river of gold, my gym is a sewer full of shit.

For this bloke, there are no jobs for the boys in diplomatic posts, board seats or manufactured public service consultancies. The Labor Party still rules, and my consistent rants against trade unions, excessive social welfare, and bloated big government haven't been forgotten. No private sector board jobs either. I'm a failed leader who, heaven forbid, lost his seat; bad for the image.

I arrive at my destination, gratefully hugging one of the flaking pillars outside my gym. Then comes an embarrassing slide to the ground accompanied by gasps and dry retching. I'm exhausted and hurting. And dreading the servitude that lies ahead.

Through the pain I notice – not for the first time – that the building facade badly needs painting. No money for that. I owe the bank a million dollars – funds I've had to borrow to buy the building – and my relationship manager, or whatever bullshit title he goes by, has stopped returning my calls.

A few hours ago, I was rudely awakened by a call from my weekend receptionist, slurring her words in between bad imitations of violent vomiting, gasping that she had gastro. Gastro? Yeah, right. Number one work excuse – especially on weekends. "How was the party last night?" She hangs up. Probably get a text resignation soon. Better off without her.

You guessed it, I'm here to open the gym doors. I've done it thousands of times. Once it used to be exhilarating; now it's drudgery. No one else to do it. Couldn't afford the extra wages anyway. No Saturday off. But at least I got my run (or shuffle) in first.

Switch on the lights, fold the towels, pick up the weights while cursing the selfish miscreants who left them on the floor, take off the pool cover, turn on the steam room, start the geriatric music; get ready for the sparrow-fart mass invasion of moaning, complaining members, all suffering from too many Friday night Cascade lagers at Knopwoods pub around the corner. I can do it in my sleep, or exhaustion – just like now.

I'm pushing sixty-five and handing out locker keys in a gym, like a Huon Valley hippie peddling weed at the Salamanca market a few metres down the street.

Help. Please. Someone. Get me out of here.

WATCH OUT FOR WANKERS

My money-guzzling gym is called Club Salamanca – to reflect its location just off Hobart's famous Salamanca Place in Battery Point on the historic boat-bejewelled working port of Sullivans Cove.

Sadly, the address is the best part. Unlike the majestic rows of nineteenth-century Georgian sandstone warehouses just metres away – now full of upmarket bars and restaurants instead of whale oil and scrimshaw – Club Salamanca hides up a dingy street at the bottom of an ugly conglomeration of fifty-six ageing apartments with all the charm of a multi-storey car park.

Even our postcode attracts heated debate. Battery Point is considered Hobart's finest suburb, with its water-lined, genteel streets of mansions belonging to the city's wealthiest families. One side of our depressing street is Battery Point (postcode 7004); the other, where we cower beneath the towering dump above, should be Hobart City (postcode 7000), but by a quirk of fate, or an inebriated town planner, has been mistakenly included in the Battery Point zone. The visual contrast is stark: the salubrious Victorian grandeur of Battery Point – and the dingy Soviet-grey shops and office blocks of the city.

I stubbornly cling to Battery Point.

"You can't use Battery Point, it's unethical," says one member, who happens to be a lawyer.

"That's a bit rich, a lawyer calling me unethical," I retort.

"Typical politician, never tell the truth. No wonder you got chucked out," he drones on. I've given up saying I'm not a politician any more. Once one, always one. I grit my teeth and carry on.

In one of my ever-increasing dark moods, I flippantly nickname the gym Club Silly Wanker – instead of Club Salamanca – and unfortunately it sticks. An unintended consequence is that members now call me the managing wanker instead of managing director. Bob Cheek MW – not MD; my fall from grace is complete.

Club Silly Wanker is supposed to be an upmarket club (I try to charge accordingly), at least for Hobart. In this case, upmarket means up-shit-creek with out-of-control costs and over-servicing creating chronic under-performance. Instead of luxuriating in the Liberal Leader's quarters in Parliament House – just a few dumbbell lunges away; in fact so close I can smell the green leather seats and watch the overpaid pollies squeeze from their chauffeur driven limos – I'm now ensconced in an office not much bigger than a broom cupboard.

I'm sick of complaints about the pool being *too* cold or *too* hot (one member, Jack, even smuggles in his own thermometer to contradict my – admittedly false – permanent 28 degree temperature chalked on the board): the steam room is always *too* steamy; the weights too old; the music *too* loud; the memberships *too* expensive. I christen it Too-Town, after Disneyland's cartoon village Toontown. This doesn't take off.

Residents in the maze of apartments above our ground-floor gym (or health and fitness club as we try to call it) never stop their tirade of abuse; one even comes down in his striped pyjamas and dressing gown each morning and storms into the gym to complain about the noise from the spa blowers. He tries to physically turn the controls off, then gets into the inevitable fight with the almost-naked members recovering from hangovers in the spa, who (encouraged by me) often threaten to drag him into the bubbling cauldron so they can drown him. That's when I get my usual morning wake-up call from the front desk: "The banana is down here again." We had taken to calling him the banana in pyjamas.

And then there's the middle-aged, normally happy lady who complains on the way out that she can't have her usual morning swim because there's someone in the pool. Someone in the pool! For Christ's sake, I patiently try to point out that the pool is 15 metres long and 8 metres wide, costs me a fortune to run, and is for the use of all members – not her bloody private lap pool. She huffs out the door.

And Bevan, bloody Bevan: suave, handsome, man-about-town, loved by all the female members, bench presses 120 kilograms, passionate Labor supporter... which means he has to bait me and appear intellectually superior at every opportunity.

"You've spelt inquiries wrong on the door; it should be enquiries," he says for the hundredth time.

"It can be either, but I've picked the American style," I patiently retort for the one-hundred and first time.

"I've just phoned Monash University and they say it has to be enquiry," he persists, more loudly this time, attracting the attention of some attractive females working out nearby.

"He's right you know," they chorus right on cue. "We've looked it up. Are you going for drinks tonight Bevo?"

Bevan beams. Hell, he's too popular for me to terminate his membership, which I'm entitled to do at any time. I resist. Inquiries is still on the door three years later. And still-a-member Bevan has just recorded his two-hundred and fiftieth assertion that it's wrong.

A former Lord Mayor of the City of Hobart lives in the penthouse above our gym. She now fills in her mostly indolent life by peering

through the window at the mall outside our front door to check that nobody ties a dog to the rusting, peeling seat she donated in memory of her late husband. One of our members, out of sheer spite and disdain for the former mayor, whom he dislikes intensely because she once knocked back a development application for his block of units, ties up not only his hound but his bike as well. He tops it off with a middle finger directed at her window. Inside, he smiles smugly as he starts his warm-up, earplugs tuned to his favourite hard-rock band, happy in the knowledge that he has successfully baited the former mayor. We wait for the inevitable phone call and torrent of abuse. It's double the volume this time.

Then there are the spoilt pretenders. One member calls himself a movie director, even though he only owns a run-down country video store that is on the verge of bankruptcy. I really don't give a stuff – but it became an issue because we had another second-rate, albeit genuine, film-producer member who took offence to what he called denigration of his industry. Give me strength. I again give up arguing that being the sole director of a company that owns a dilapidated video store selling mainly R-rated videos and DVDs doesn't mean he can say he's a "movie director".

Not to mention Liverpudlian Lenny. I inherited Lenny from a previous gym of mine, Dockside. He was one of the Liverpool orphans who came to Australia just after the war, and he still prattled nonsense in a Beatles Merseyside accent at breakneck speed. He told me he just wanted to do odd jobs around the place – pottering around in the plant room – in return for soaking in the spa (and ogling the girls). Try as I might to lose him, he discovered Club Silly Wanker and adopted it as his new home.

"Isn't he great offering to work for nothing in return, just time in the spa?" gushed the members.

"He breaks everything he touches," I moaned. "Wish he'd stayed in Liverpool."

Secretly, I liked Lenny. Strangely, though, he always came to the gym in bare feet, even in winter.

"You're not going into the gym like that, Lenny. Wear some bloody shoes," I chided. "You're not in Liverpool now."

When I warned the front desk girls about Lenny's podiatry nakedness they looked surprised. "He's always in expensive Reeboks when we see him," they said. Indeed. Lenny always arrived in bare feet but he left in trendy designer shoes. He had discovered the Lost and Found basket out the back and helped himself to a different pair before leaving every night. At least it explained my ritual daily fights with members who accused me of selling their lost shoes to make some money.

"I'm not responsible for your sneakers if you're stupid enough to leave them behind," I told them. "They smell like a sewerage plant anyway. Who'd want them?"

Lenny did. He protested that he was taking them home to clean them.

As usual, I gave up. Lenny's still in the spa. Now, after he does a job, I just offer him the Lost and Found basket as a lucky dip.

God knows I've tried to further improve the club. I developed a Pilates studio over the road, expanded into the computer store next door, and installed an expensive spray-tan booth. Spray tan! Oh, Jesus, great move, that one. More of that later.

I invited Heather, one of the country's top Pilates teachers, to train our staff before opening our studio. As it happened, construction got behind schedule and the place looked like a bombsite when she arrived. One of our staff, I'll call her Anna, had just had a baby but still wanted to come. Heather denied her entry because the site was too dangerous for a pram-bound baby. Anna took to social media to complain, and in solidarity all my instructors went on strike. Members left in droves as a protest against sexism. And I got the blame, not bloody Heather.

I later forgave her and invited her to open the new Pilates studio before a healthy turnout of our members (you owe me, Heather, I said).

Now, admittedly the studio was jam-packed and Heather's lectern was rather fragile (hired cheaply for the night). I introduced her as Australia's leading Pilates teacher (she was probably not in the top fifty, but who cares, we're in Tassie). Rapturous applause. Heather got up and started gulping for air like a goldfish out of its tank.

"For Christ's sake say something," I whisper. "I paid your travel expenses to come here. The media are covering this."

She gulps some more – and then runs out of the room. I run after her.

"I can't do it," she sobs. "They're all standing so close to me."

I give up, and go back to apologise, saying Heather's not feeling well. I call for drinks to be served to appease the masses. Next thing I know, Heather is there with a glass of wine in hand, happily sipping away. She even sent me a bill for her attendance.

Oh yes, the spray-tan disaster. In desperation I ordered a private, do-it-yourself spray-tan booth to cater to Hobart's "beautiful people". Competitive advantage, upmarket club and all that. It cost me $68,000. Staff training was an issue, with part-time receptionists being called on to change liquids and give instructions to users. I couldn't afford anyone to run it full-time.

Anyway, to cut a long story short, all was going well until a wedding party arranged to have a spray tan the day before their big event. The receptionist must have been off sick on spray training day and had missed a crucial part of the course, because the bride emerged looking like a brown-and-white zebra.

"Jesus Christ, what have you done?" I quizzed her.

"I forgot to clean the pipes," she confessed. I should have given her a verbal spray – but I didn't. Words failed me. My insurance premiums sky-rocketed after that.

The spray-tan wreck lay rusting in its custom-built room for many years – a monument to its owner's stupidity and the fact that he couldn't bear to face up to his failures. Eventually, a builder mate, Wayne, came in with his sledgehammer and took the pulped remains to the Hobart tip – but not before the indignant booth took its final revenge.

To his horror, Wayne discovered there was still liquid in the pipes as he sliced into the morass of connections... and he emerged covered in golden spray – clothes and all. It was Gold Coast perfect – first time ever. Wayne had the spa control panel framed and mounted, and it's now on my office wall with an inscribed warning: "Life is too short to make the wrong decision twice." It continues to haunt me.

And then there were the entirely unnecessary expensive chairs. My staff insisted I get in an interior designer for the Silly Wanker extensions and upgrade ("Gotta do it right, Bob") and, of course, we had to have over-priced, ornate, crystal-looking, fragile chairs with decorative arm rests – more at home in Buckingham Palace than in a gym. They survived unscathed until the introduction of sales manager Meg's weight loss program in the run-up to the Hobart Cup. She had all the overweight, scallop-pie-scoffing and champagne-swilling Battery Point residents well and truly under her spell – and, more importantly, paying big dollars for the promise of shoehorning into new dresses and suits for the big event on the Tasmanian social calendar.

Money spinner, it was. And I say was. One day, a rather portly matron, wife of an influential businessman, succumbed to Meg's spiel, signed up to the program, and then rose from her Buckingham Palace chair – or at least tried to. Most observers described her appearance as that of a tortoise, with the palace chair stuck firmly to her ample posterior. The chairs are now in storage. And so is the weight loss program.

One member, I'll call him Harry, uses the gym to shower and shave each morning, even if he doesn't work out, like it was his own private bathroom. I only found out when an interstate mutual friend stayed at Harry's suburban home and was told to stow his luggage in the shower, because he uses the one at Club Salamanca. I fronted Harry. "Mate, it's a gym, not a bloody private ablutions parlour," I said. "You have a workout, then shower and go home." No wonder I can't afford to pay the power bill.

The Liberal Premier was jammed in by the secretary of the Tasmanian branch of the ACTU, the local Greens Senator and, worse, a local businessman who had just been hit by a hike in land tax.

Another genius lathered up and shaved in the steam room, theatrically shaking out his razor after each sweep of the jaw line – much to the disgust of his fellow steamers, especially the females.

Rumour around town is that if you want to know what's happening in Hobart you just go to the Club Silly Wanker steam room. The puffs of vapour and violent sweating loosens tongues so that members reveal who they're sleeping with and what happened on the recent trip to Thailand.

We had a coup when the Tasmanian Premier joined. Unfortunately, he chose to go to the steam room after his workout – and even worse, he sat on the inside of the bottom bench, which holds four. This is the "no-go" zone because if anyone you don't like comes in and sits beside you there's no escape. The Liberal Premier was jammed in by the secretary of the Tasmanian branch of the ACTU, the local Greens Senator and, worse, a local businessman who had just been hit by a hike in land tax.

Mr Premier escaped an hour later. It was five minutes before closing, just enough time to cancel his membership before stepping into his chauffeured limo and heading to his home gym.

Only last night, one of Hobart's more prominent lawyers had been working up speed on the treadmill towards the end of his run, when his spectacles dropped off his nose onto the floor. So, you stop the treadmill, retrieve the glasses, then resume your run, right? Oh, no.

This intellectual giant continues running, gradually bending his knees like a waddling duck, and attempts to pick up his glasses off the floor without breaking stride.

The result was like an Olympic diver realising halfway through his final attempt from the 10 metre tower that he's not going to make it: an out-of-control, double-backward-flip head smash into the glass office window behind. Result? Nose fractured, forehead cut, blood all over the carpet and, when he eventually wakes up, the threat of blood all over the courtroom floor. Mine. Not enough clearance between the Life Fitness treadie and the office, he bellows, while waiting for the ambulance. Not surprisingly, he doesn't like being called a dickhead for not hitting the stop button. Barrister injured in gym. All over. Just write the cheque now. Why couldn't he have been a mild-mannered office assistant?

Just as I thought the chaotic scene of blood and carnage and legal threats couldn't get any worse, Jack emerged from the pool carrying his dripping thermometer: "It's only 23 degrees – not 28. You've lied again," he smirks. "I've rubbed out your number on the board and put in mine."

I explode. "Go and change it back or I'll bloody kill you," I roar. "And your membership is terminated as of now." I know I'm within my rights under the terms of the membership contract. But shit, that's $1,200 a year I've just lost. Worth it, I reason, to get rid of the prick.

The dazed and bloodied lawyer, propped up against the treadmill, summons the strength to call Jack over. Whispers and pointing in my direction follow. Not one – but two – claims for damages end up on my desk.

Yes, I'm definitely Bob the Managing Wanker; trying to make money from a gym full of wankers. No chance.

ALWAYS "SIGN THE CHEQUES" YOURSELF

was pressed into the gym game by chance. I'd always had some interest in weight training and, as a skinny kid, bought Joe Weider's mail-order chest expander and hand squeezers in a desperate attempt to put some meat on my bones. Then, when I was about sixteen, I hopped on a train from the family farm at Evandale to Hobart – a 400-kilometre round trip – and bought a set of barbells and dumbbells from Bridges Brothers in Elizabeth Street.

I used to do bench presses and squats in the back shed, resting the bar on two 44 gallon petrol drums and using Mum's heavily carved Chinese camphor chest as a bench. The result was a perfect red-raw tattoo of a Chinese temple and mandarins on my back after every

If you have no control over how and why the business is spending money, you'll almost certainly fail.

workout; stress for my mother, who feared I was dead every time the barbell missed the drums and crashed to the floor; and heaps of injuries from poor form and improvised props. And alas, after all the effort, I still looked like soup bones. I was forever known by my mates as "streak of misery", "beanpole" or "chopsticks", some telling me "you'd make a good pull-through for a rifle".

But my primitive interest in weights was driven by my obsession with sport and becoming a champion footballer – not by wanting to be a gym owner. That was fate.

Most successful business and life decisions can be reduced to two words: timing and luck. But you also have to keep trying; if you do, those two magic words will eventually fall in your favour. For instance, my timing on a new gym concept was spot-on; but trying to develop a building into apartments that I part-owned in Hunter Street, Hobart, was disastrous, because we did it during the economic downturn of the late 1990s. We were forced to sell everything, including our plans. And guess what! Just as we did, the property market in Hobart took off. The new developer used our model to build what is now the Zero One apartment complex and, presumably, to make a fortune, while we were left to pay off hundreds of thousands of dollars in debt. Yep, it was timing – good for him, bad for us – and luck.

Being introduced to modern gyms in the early 1980s – as distinct from the sweat-and-liniment, male-only, iron-pumping dungeons of days gone by – also taught me one of the most important lessons in business: Always sign the cheques yourself (or in this digital age, always authorise online banking transactions yourself). If you have no control over how and why the business is spending money, you'll almost certainly fail.

When I retired from Tasmanian Football League club Clarence in 1975 I was a journalist working for *The Mercury* newspaper in Hobart (it's still owned by Rupert Murdoch, although I doubt he knows it). I loved being a newspaper reporter but, after a stint working in Queenstown on Tassie's remote and rugged West Coast, I arrived back in Hobart desperate to invest in some sort of business; a journalist's wage just wouldn't meet the needs of a growing family.

Some of my footy mates went into owning pubs. I liked a drink, but the smell of stale beer and cigarettes wasn't for me, let alone chucking out drunks at closing time.

Former Geelong and North Hobart footy champion John Devine, fondly known as JD and a successful hotelier, confirmed my view of pubs when he yarned about his ongoing problems with troublemakers – especially at one notorious establishment known as The Bloodhouse on Hobart's Eastern Shore – and how he solved the problem. The strategy was to lend one of these nuisances, let's call him Mick, $50 (Mick had a gambling problem). A few nights later, JD would go into the bar and bellow, for all to hear: "Where's that bastard Mick? He owes me $50." Mick was never seen again.

In 1980, I was on a Sunday morning footy show on local TV, famous for one hour of hangover-charged, mistake-riddled nonsense. One of my fellow panellists was Hawthorn goal-kicking legend Peter Hudson, who owned the Granada Tavern at Berriedale and was the coach of league side Glenorchy. He at least added some respectability to the comedy hour. After the show, we'd often relax with a few beers and a barbecue at the back of the TV studio. One Sunday, "Huddo" mentioned that he and JD were buying into the new Lifestyle health and fitness club that had just opened in a prime location on Hobart's waterfront. Lifestyle was a pioneering chain of fitness clubs founded by champion distance runner Ron Clarke – who lit the flame at the 1956 Melbourne Olympics and held several world records – and his Melbourne business partner, Terry Moore.

Alas, the trail-blazing concept wasn't looking so promising and Clarke and Moore were keen to reduce their stake in the business. When they found someone eager to buy, they couldn't believe their luck. They reluctantly retained 50 per cent after flogging off the other half to a very hairy former navy pilot, nicknamed Waxo because he spent most of his time getting his back hair removed.

Waxo's lack of business acumen was matched only by his dearth of fitness knowledge. The founders now wanted out completely – to beat the liquidator as they watched the increasingly falling revenue with great alarm. Along came JD and Huddo, who picked up 40 per cent for virtually nothing (it was a punt for these two, who had already made millions from pubs).

After a lifetime of sport and trying to stay fit, it piqued my interest, and I said I might consider coming in on the act. Huddo mentioned that Clarke may be "persuaded" to sell another 5 per cent if I asked nicely.

I must have been extremely nice, because Clarke took all of ten seconds to offer me 5 per cent for $5,000 (I wondered why he was sighing over the phone; as I found out later, it was relief). It may not seem like much today, but $5,000 was a fortune for me at that stage of my life. Ron also offered me his position on the board, which I thought was an incredible gesture, and to top it off I'd get directors' fees. I was too naive to know I'd just taken over his guarantee and responsibilities for Lifestyle Hobart. The fees lasted all of one month; the company just couldn't afford to pay them.

The predictions were optimistic, but it was early days. I soon learned the fledgling Australian fitness industry already had a frightening reputation. A twelve-month membership was normally about $150 upfront, and you hoped to hell the poor unsuspecting victim never came back to take hot showers and push up the power bill, let alone get fit. Cancellations were made almost impossible; and money back? – no chance!

I plead guilty that at first I followed the script and insisted that any quitting member come in personally to sign a cancellation form – that is, until one member with a broken arm and leg was wheeled in by a distressed wife – screaming "Where's that bastard Bob Cheek?" The poor accident victim had to scrawl his signature with his non-preferred left hand. I half-heartedly joked to my alarmed staff that we'd have to get him back because I couldn't decipher the scribble. There were no laughs. Enough was enough. I reluctantly exempted badly injured (or dying) members – as long as they could produce medical certificates, of course.

In the beginning treadmills were virtually unknown, as was all modern-day electronic equipment. Gyms kept costs down by having massive Jane Fonda–inspired aerobics rooms and huge free-weight sections... all to compensate for unsanitary pools, spas, steam rooms and saunas. Aerobics confused the population in the 1980s. The DJ at one local radio station kept referring to it as "acrobatics" – until I phoned in to say "We're a gym, not a bloody circus" (although that assertion was open to dispute).

Unscrupulous operators abounded. Most were charlatans who spent the money as soon as they could get their grubby little hands on it, and never had enough to keep the gym running. One notorious Western Australian gym operator sold life, yes life, memberships for as little as $125 just before he went broke. Others offered five years for $55. But governments seemed reluctant to act as more cases of swindling appeared.

Nightly TV screens were full of finance companies repossessing gym equipment and lugging it out the door, followed by owners mouthing obscenities as they tried to halt the carnage. Viewers loved the drama. It was reality TV way ahead of its time. One repossession posse in Melbourne even brought along its own snarling Dobermans as they heaved weight stacks down the stairs (the owner thought it was safer to be on the first floor). Bad move: no escape.

But while the public loved the nightly TV drama, it did very little for selling memberships and, after a few months, I sensed that Lifestyle Hobart was headed for the same fate. I sought a meeting with Waxo – the 50 per cent shareholder and managing director – who still had his pilot's licence (we joked he had a plane at Hobart Airport ready to fly him to Argentina if the crunch came). Later, I realised it was no joke.

I also tentatively asked in advance if I could possibly see the monthly profit and losses, budgets and balance sheets. After all, I was a director and – albeit a very small – shareholder. If you wouldn't mind, please; I know it's a very unusual request.

This proposition was met with great alarm. Initially the lunchtime board meetings – always held in the subleased Italian restaurant that was part of the building – started with a glass of chianti and the ritual of handing out the director fee cheques (before they bounced), hopefully creating a mood of great conviviality and leading to a "who cares about the gym" mentality after the last glass of grappa at 5pm.

I'd already had to cough up far more than $5,000 to cover guarantees called in by banks, equipment companies, and whoever else had been silly enough to believe in the Lifestyle Hobart story. Waxo, flanked by one of his steroid-filled meatheads masquerading as bodybuilders, listened to my complaints in silence, eyes flashing like two billionaire's engagement rings – unfortunately with fury, not love. The request for up-to-date financial data finished him off. Waxo's trademark hair bristled as he threatened to drown me in the spa and then decompose my body in the sauna before tossing the remains into the harbour. As punishment, he angrily wrote out a cheque for $5,000 and told me to get out and never come back.

Oh, and as further punishment I was no longer a director. Thank you, Waxo. Although it took me months to get my name off all the guarantees, I couldn't believe my luck. I banked this cheque within minutes. And, amazingly, it didn't bounce. I immediately went to a waterfront pub and celebrated with all the drunks. I even lent some money to one of them – just to help JD and Huddo's cashflow.

Shortly after my lucky escape, it was Lifestyle Hobart's turn on the nightly news. Waxo and several of his meatheads were seen vainly grappling with security men as they marched down the corridor with the precious treadmill, benches and weights to the waiting removalist vans. There were no dogs, and Waxo had no first-floor sanctuary. The building was repossessed and, when the doors finally closed, nearly a thousand members, who had paid upfront fees, were left with empty pockets and without a gym. By this time, Waxo's wing tips were just a sparkle in the sky as he headed into the wide blue yonder.

Several months later, backed by a group of friends, I negotiated with the equipment financiers, the bank and the building owner, tourism guru Lloyd Clark, to reopen the business under a new name, Dockside.

It took time to regain control. The pool was like a frog pond: green and covered with slime after months of neglect; dirt and dust covered the ghost-like rooms; and the stench of long-gone steroid-fuelled bodybuilders was a reminder of all that was wrong with the industry. I persevered and radically changed the way the club operated, introducing pay-by-the-month memberships and educating the city's residents on the benefits of health and fitness. I eventually rebuilt Dockside into one of Australia's most successful gyms, with a membership exceeding 3,000.

I was managing director. And, yes, I was signing the cheques.

CURIOSITY KILLS CATS, NOT HUMANS

The health-and-fitness industry is the only one in the world that charges people to work – well, work out at least. What a concept. Usually, it's the other way around and workers get paid by the owners. Imagine, say, a construction company making people pay for the privilege of slaving away on a jackhammer or lumping bricks around on a building site.

"Me pay you?" the foreman would say at day's end. "Mate, you owe me $10 for a casual visit."

This really has nothing to do with my story, except to again highlight what a unique industry I worked in. And how surprises lurked around every corner. For instance, what other business would be built on the tradition of working out in the nude, as was the ancient Greek gymnasium? (Although, apparently, leather pouches were available at the front desk for the more shy and retiring Greek gent, the same way we sell T-shirts and towels. And that's right: women in ancient Greece didn't frequent gyms.)

Thankfully, nobody attempted to work out nude in *my* gyms; although, there was the time an elderly member, Jim, willed his arthritis-racked body into the Dockside pool area for an early morning swim and slowly, painfully, removed his 1940s vintage-green tracksuit. He struggled upright – relieved to straighten his cracking old bones and looking forward to toppling into the warm (28 degrees, of course) water – only to be deafened by a crescendo of female screams the like of which our gym had never heard before.

Not only did the shrieks confirm our modern mixed-gender status, and that the pool was packed, but they also woke our attendant dozing behind the recently removed covers after a big night partying. To her credit, she remained calm.

"I think you've forgotten something, Jim," she intoned softly. He had: his swimming costume. Unfortunately, we were all out of leather pouches. Alerted by the chaos, I escorted Jim, now shrouded in two fluffy white Dockside embroidered towels, back to the change rooms.

In 2007, the fitness industry was pouring out more gyms than an over-worked barista pours caffeine shots – mostly big, over-capitalised and over-serviced edifices with pools and spas, expensive tiles and solid mahogany reception desks. Strange, really, because the barriers to entry are so low – the so-called narrow moat in business terms – that virtually anyone can lease a shed, toss in some hired second-hand equipment and call it a gym. Before going broke. I labelled them Palaces of the Poor – or POPs for short: poorly designed but, most importantly, guaranteed to turn the owners (and I suspect some over-charged members) into paupers. Never mind about making a profit.

Perhaps that's why entrepreneurs wanted to build fitness-centre Taj Mahals: to gain prestige and notoriety. Before going broke, but in a bigger way (owing more money). For most, it was an ego trip:

former aerobics instructors, personal trainers and gym members, with no business sense and plenty of borrowed money, plunging into the sweat-stained world of barbells and bastardry. And, hey, where else can you be photographed with a hot-bod personal trainer and run around in a gym "business suit" of tight shorts and T-shirt while calling yourself the Boss?

Over-servicing was rife. People just wanted to say they provided better service than anyone else. We had so many testimonials to say how fantastic we were and we won the best customer service award on radio Triple R (R for Ridiculous).

To make matters worse, in my town, Hobart, local government had started to build the palaces and use ratepayers' money to take on private enterprise. For them, profit and putting hard-working gym owners out of business was the least of their worries; getting re-elected was far more important. And no problem if we don't have a surplus (local government word for profit); we'll just slug the unsuspecting ratepayers a bit more. On top of this, newly installed institutes and training academies were siphoning off taxpayers' money to turn out conveyor-belts-full of personal trainers and instructors who had next to no business experience and would never pay back their student loans.

But still hopefuls opened gyms... or maybe marbled personal training studios... and offered fabulous service. Cool, eh?

In Australia, virtually no-one thought to own more than one gym and create a chain: or even to franchise. Of the ones who did, all failed through lack of funds and inexperience. The consensus was to put all of your resources into one spectacular muscled mausoleum and make it the best. They forgot that gyms are gyms; people just want results – bigger biceps and toned butts and abs – not hordes of instructors interrupting their workouts to ask how they're going. ("Yeah I'm great. Now fuck off so I can finish my routine.") Or owners and managers ringing them to find out why they haven't been attending the gym regularly. ("Really? Thanks for reminding me that I haven't been in for three months. Just cancel my membership if I haven't been using it.")

Sorry folks, whether you like it or not, gyms rely on people paying even when they're not using the facilities; if they paid by the visit, you'd be getting the dole in no time. So, don't remind them.

Among this carnage, I realised the Club Silly Wanker model had to change.

We were charging each member a $330 joining fee; then $55.90 a fortnight, regardless of what they used. People who used the pool, spa and steam room were charged the same as those who didn't. We had to cover the huge power costs of the palace. And then we kicked them out at 9pm. Oh, and on Sundays it was 4pm, after opening at a lazy 9am. "Don't complain, you ungrateful pests, we can't afford the penalty rates at weekends."

I was mulling over this problem – how to increase hours without a cost blowout – when the latest edition of the monthly IHRSA magazine landed in my Sandy Bay home letterbox. IHRSA stands for the quaintly named International Health and Racquetball Sports Association – an amalgam of disparate American sports bodies that had now become the world's leading gym organisation. The annual IHRSA convention attracted more than 12,000 wide-eyed attendees from all over the planet.

I'd made a point of joining IHRSA – when I could ill afford the steep US-dollar annual fee and only a handful of Aussie gyms were members – because the glossy magazine kept me in touch with what was happening around the globe. The few Aussie gyms that did receive the mag all the way from IHRSA's Boston headquarters were either too arrogant to read it because they reckoned they knew everything; or too busy trying to make ends meet in their POP.

I was losing money, too, but I would still read the mag late at night after a 12-hour day – in the desperate hope I could change my fortunes. This particular night, though, having received the latest tome, I decided I was too tired. I'll look at it tomorrow morning, I thought, between yawns. But as it turned out, I couldn't resist having a casual flick, Milo and Teddy Bear biscuit supper in hand, through the pages containing

Never think you know it all.
Be a stickybeak. Look around
yourself and learn. Keep your eyes
and ears wide open.

the usual well-meaning but often mindless advice. There were also the usual stories of American gym owners pontificating on why their clubs were superior to everyone else's, even though they weren't profitable. Not much this month, I concluded.

But then... I came to the last few pages. Little did I know that those precious back five pages would change my life forever. And that most people wouldn't have read them.

Among the myriad last-minute equipment adverts was a small section that listed new members of IHRSA. Usually this was a handful of American Midwest newcomers with imaginative names like "Jim's Gym" or "Nebraska New-Body", all doomed to fail, in my opinion. But, shit, this month the list ran to, geezus, bloody hundreds. The names tumbled down the page! I was blinded by the kaleidoscope of new clubs – in just about every American state.

What the hell was going on? It was the start of the 24-hour small-box gym revolution, that's what. (Small-box gyms – usually open plan and no more than 400 square metres – never closed 24/7 and had unlimited key entry, unlike the then-normal multi-roomed large gyms with restricted hours.)

I squeezed the page to my chest as if it was a newborn baby.

This was my chance... my last chance... *Take it Bob, please. Just take it.* I didn't sleep that night. Too excited.

It was early 2008, with the global financial crisis in full swing, and I squeezed my over-worked credit card for a last-ditch return airfare to Los Angeles, flying economy with Qantas. Little did I know it would be the last time I would fly down the back of a plane.

Suddenly I felt young again. And, because I was curious about what was going on in other parts of the world, I was about to surf the wave of a lifetime. A magic carpet – or should I say rubberised mat – to riches beyond my wildest dreams.

Never think you know it all. Be a stickybeak. Look around yourself and learn. Keep your ears and eyes wide open; don't be a tin-eared and eyes-closed loser. You can even call it intellectual inquisitiveness if it makes you feel better.

Curiosity may kill cats... but never humans. Only arrogance does that.

EVERYONE NEEDS A MEGASTAR

've always had a good feel for numbers – numerate is the word – without being an accountant. At school, in the days before calculators, my party trick was to ask people to throw any figures at me in quick succession, from thousands to millions, in any arithmetical equation, and I'd come up with the right answer.

Family and friends used to trot me out at any gathering under the banner "Robert the Human Calculator" – or later I was simply "Rapid-Fire Robert" – like some freak show at a circus. They'd spend what seemed hours beforehand laboriously totalling up the numbers they were going to chuck at me – to make sure I gave the right answer. I never failed.

My reward was usually a glass of Mum's homemade ginger beer or some hot, buttered pikelets. My elder brother and sister were smarter –

they took bets that I couldn't come up with the right answer – and made enough for a new 45 RPM vinyl disc by Johnny Ray or The Platters. It was a sad day when modern calculators were invented and Rapid-Fire Robert went the same way as the silent movie stars.

In business, the ability to do the numbers in your head while negotiating deals is invaluable. It's also good to have a feel for whether a venture will make money – without resorting to endless spreadsheets, budgets and business plans.

As a former journalist, I also had some flair for marketing, promotion and branding; knew a bit about the fitness industry; loved negotiating deals; and took pride in my work. But there was one area in which I knew I had a glaring weakness – sales. And without sales in the fitness industry, you might as well stay in bed and dream about opening your own business.

It wasn't as though I hadn't tried: I'd sold ferrets, Muscovy ducks and broken-down sheep dogs in Tasmania's Cooee saleyards when I was a young trainee stock agent/auctioneer; flogged insurance when I first came to Hobart to play football for Clarence (the only two policies I sold were to my father-in-law and myself); and Scotch sticky tape and scouring pads for American company 3M around Tassie's supermarkets and newsagencies in the early 1970s. All with little success. The 3M company even made the mistake of flying me to Sydney for a comprehensive, two-week sales training course – but all I learned was how to smoke my first joints, party all night after watching *Hair*, and compare life in the city of free love to life in Hobart. I left soon after – telling everyone I couldn't "stick to" the job.

If necessary, I could sell a membership if someone walked through the gym door, but I'd anxiously seek help, and would only take on the task if none was forthcoming. I didn't have the patience or empathy to find out why people wanted to join. That was for the rare few in this world who were born to sell.

In human resource terms, the basic starting point for success in fitness start-ups is one person with some business smarts and another

The basic starting point for success in fitness start-ups is one person with some business smarts and another who can sell Japanese whale meat to the Sea Shepherd crew.

who can sell Japanese whale meat to the Sea Shepherd crew. Sadly, most people have neither.

The fitness industry treats prospective members as complete fools by labelling salespeople as "membership consultants" or "fitness coaches" or "team fitness" or "care team". Mate, call 'em what you like, but they're there to sell you a membership.

TRIGGER WARNING: Stop reading here if you're in sales.

Dynamic salespeople are a nightmare to handle. They pay no attention to detail; are rarely on time; blow up at the slightest provocation; take days off for stress leave if they don't make targets; and will cut corners to achieve results. But good ones are worth the effort. You can't do without them.

Welcome back all salespeople – you can continue reading now.

I nailed the magic human resource duo when I teamed with a woman called Suzie to resurrect the failed Lifestyle gym under the new name Dockside. Diminutive Suzie had worked there part-time but departed as the ironically named Lifestyle slowly turned into Dead Duck. She wasn't to blame. I wanted her back.

We had an enthralling love–hate relationship, a bit like skippering a double kayak in the Sydney-to-Hobart yacht race, but we made it work. Suzie resigned seven times – and came back six. (When she cracked one last time she went to my opposition around the corner. They did eventually go broke, but Suzie had left long before that happened.)

One time, shortly after her resignation, she rang me from hospital while having her anaesthetic before an operation. The conversation went like this: "You bloody bastard, I hate you, can't stand you, so glad I've left... hate you, hate you..." Then the phone went dead as she passed out. See what I mean? Believe it or not, we're still good friends. And she worked on my second successful political campaign years later, when I topped the poll in my electorate of Denison.

In one extraordinary act during the campaign, Suzie negotiated to put one of my giant banners on a previously untouchable block of flats in the middle of a working-class Labor suburb; but it covered the dining room window of one, and the tenants weren't happy. She talked them into lighting candles during the day for romantic lunches! Suzie was a real winner.

I wasn't so lucky at Club Silly Wanker. Jazzer wasn't too bad as a sales manager, but I made the mistake of trying to promote her to acting general manager while I went on a long-overdue holiday. I took her for coffee to give her the good news, but the reaction didn't go to plan. She looked at me in absolute horror. It was a look that said: "You mean I've got to be responsible for this dump and the shitty members and actually do some work?" Two weeks later, she resigned and I cancelled my holiday. That was when I learned that most salespeople don't make good GMs.

I tried several salespeople after that. One turned out to be an alcoholic; when he showed up for work with safety pins in his white shirt instead of buttons, and he took lunch at 9.30am, I knew I was in trouble. I was getting desperate. Sales were plummeting.

It was late one afternoon at Club Silly Wanker. Slow day. No sales. I was on the front desk handling the usual member complaints when a wide-eyed, wild-haired woman clad in Nike joggers and polo shirt pierced my dark mood with an outstretched hand.

"Hi, I'm Meg," she said. "And I'm here to sell you fitness equipment." I laughed. Meg worked for a large Melbourne fitness equipment distribution firm that I didn't deal with and was in town with her boss to try to sell me some of her products. Fat chance.

"They told me not to bother coming to see you because you deal with another firm," she said matter-of-factly. "But I bet them I'd get you to buy some of our stuff."

Two days of charm, Inane chatter, and a seafood dinner at Mures later, I did. Fifteen Le Monde spin bikes, to be precise – the first ever order I'd given to Meg's company. I had so enjoyed the banter that I couldn't even remember signing the order form.

Good salespeople have the knack of making you talk about yourself – feel good about yourself – and she had little problem with someone who tended to err on the side of egotism. "Oh, really?" is their approach. "You didn't?" and "How good is that!"

I had to have this girl on my team. But why would she want to leave a good job in Melbourne to work at Club Silly Wanker? In the end, she decided she wanted a sea change. I had no idea how I would pay the generous salary I offered, or the new car I promised. I think I even said BMW... which turned into a second-hand Toyota Corolla. We worked together to try to resurrect Club Silly Wanker, and that was when I decided to extend into the former computer store next door. More money and more heartache.

Meg's sales skills were amazing – but she had the usual super salesperson's lack of attention to detail. And punctuality was non-existent. "Where the bloody hell are ya?" became my mobile catchcry, as the deadline for a meeting rolled well past start time. Early on, she told me the story about how a previous sales manager had given her a lift to work every day. "What a good bloke," I said. "That's really nice." I soon realised the reason: to get her to work on time.

Super sellers will do anything – anything – to make targets. I believed in incentives and offered Meg $10,000 if she could achieve a total of 1,000 members at Club Silly Wanker by a certain date. At the start of the last week, the situation looked hopeless – she needed another 150 and her average was ten a week. I refused to discount fees to get the extra members, despite Megastar's pleas, and turned to other important matters in the knowledge my ten grand was safe.

I was sitting at home, watching the telly on the last Sunday night, when I got an excited phone call. Megastar had turned into Megabucks. "We made target," she gushed. "Bullshit!" I said, "That's impossible." She was adamant. I drove in to Club Silly Wanker to check. Sure enough, our computers showed 1,001 members.

"Can I have the $10,000 tomorrow?" she said.

"What's the hurry?"

"I have things to buy."

On the Monday morning, I went through every sale. We had gained 200 over the weekend – unprecedented. But, hey, hang on a minute, they all worked for the Tasmanian electricity retailer Aurora Energy. What was odd, though, was that the entire eligible Aurora workforce was fewer than 200.

I didn't much like corporate sales or discounts for major employers. Usually they guarantee that lots of their workforce will join – but mostly it works out to be about 10 per cent. However, Aurora had its headquarters just over the road from the Wanker – so I made an exception. When I had refused to give Meg any discounts, she had racked her brains on how she could meet the target. The Aurora discount... the shining light! So she rang up all her leads and offered them Aurora rates – hoping I wouldn't notice.

Meg didn't get her bonus. On principle, I should have sacked her. Instead I settled for a stern lecture on ethics. Deep down, I liked her determination to meet target, but not at any cost. And where else was I going to get someone who could sell like Meg? Expediency won the day. There were no more corporate sales.

Despite our best efforts, the Wanker still yanked dollars out of my pocket into an endless array of power bills, wages, repairs and failed attempts to try something new. Anything. Then, in mid-2007, Meg quit to travel. She'd had enough of the never-ending grind and pressure of a business going nowhere. Despite our combined efforts, the 2006/07 accounts had shown a loss of $37,003.

I needed Meg back: the formula of "business brain + sales supremo =

success" remained the key fitness industry ratio. We just needed a new avenue.

By early 2008 I had tracked Meg down in London and enticed her back – this time with the promise of a Kombi van so she could go camping, and the additional promise that I would stop saying "Where the bloody hell are ya?" and let her run her own race.

As luck would have it, the IHRSA magazine had just arrived. So I also promised her an economy return trip to the United States – to accompany me in my search for the holy grail of fitness – and my redemption from political failure.

THE NAME OF
THE GAME IS
THE NAME

The intrepid Aussie forward scouts – all two of them – descended into the Los Angeles smog in early March 2008, excited and intent on sussing out the sprinkle of 24-hour gyms that had bloomed like cactus flowers across California.

I felt a bit like Ray Kroc in the 1950s when he heard about a new-fangled fast-food restaurant run by the McDonald brothers in nearby San Bernardino and drove across the American continent to find out what was going on. Being curious made the Macca's founder a few billion; hell, just a few million would do me.

We needed wheels. Shrugging off the cramped, economy-inspired, sleepless fifteen-hour flight, not to mention the jet lag, I hired a Mustang convertible (what else, in California?) and with the Beach Boys blasting out on the car radio (also what else, in California?) to keep us awake, we hurtled down the coast to San Diego, purportedly to the site of a new small-box gym.

It was a warm Sunday morning when we pulled up at the nondescript office-type building on the outskirts of the city. "Damn, I forgot it was Sunday morning," I said to Meg. "It'll probably be closed."

"Not if it's really 24 hours," she reminded me. Correct. There were people happily working out, even though the door was closed. We tried to open it – to no avail. So we knocked, loudly. Eventually a member, Randy, opened the door.

"Forgotten your key, buddy," he said to me. Then, glancing across to Meg, "Are you members?"

I tried to explain, not very convincingly, that we were Aussie gym owners checking out our American cousins. Randy didn't believe a word and moved to close the door with a "Sorry, guys."

"Hey, man, don't lock out a fellow American," Meg interjected in her best New Yorker accent. "I've only been down under for a coupla years and just want to soak up some American culture again."

And so ensued a conversation as long as the Brooklyn Bridge about everything from street dogs to Barack Obama and Grimaldi's pizzas. All bullshit and "you got-its" and hundreds of "guys" – but I was saved by the super salesgirl again.

Randy, literally eating popcorn and pretzels out of Meg's hand, not only let us in but showed us around and explained how the gym operated. I listened in suspended animation, entranced. Only staffed about forty hours a week; members let themselves in with keys after hours; low cost; basic equipment without pools, spas or silver service; and, most importantly, open 24 hours, 7 days a week. Rapid-Fire Robert did the figures in his head – and beamed.

Randy babbled on, spilling the chilli beans. We couldn't stop him once he started – not that we tried. Revolutionary; taking America by storm; the next big thing... the words dripped from his lips like rainwater onto a drought-gripped sheep farm.

"You need a franchise though," Randy said, suddenly serious. "There's a sophisticated security system this guy has invented when members come through the door. It's a lot harder than it looks. Franchises are springing up everywhere. Not sure if they're in Australia yet."

I couldn't care less. I hated franchises anyway.

"You'll also get into trouble if you let people in the door without a key. I shouldn't have let you guys in. Hope I don't get found out. Don't tell anyone."

Sorry, Randy, too late.

After swiping as many different pamphlets and as much other info as we could, we thanked Randy and left. Outside, Meg and I looked at each other, burst out laughing and gave each other an impromptu high five before doing what could only be described as an Aussie rap dance. We were onto something big here. Big. Big. We both knew it.

The next 24-hour club on our list was in Pasadena, north-west of Los Angeles. This time, naturally, the Mustang radio reverberated with Jan and Dean's classic "The Little Old Lady from Pasadena" – while I argued, vehemently but incorrectly, that it was by the Beach Boys – as we retraced our miles back to LA and beyond.

We lucked out. Unbeknown to us, we'd been caught on camera entering the San Diego club without authority – and, as we soon discovered, poor old Randy was in big trouble. Word was out: look out for two Aussie Bonnie and Clyde types terrorising Californian gyms. At least we knew the security system worked.

The Pasadena gym was staffed. And the franchisee–owner opened the door with a smile that faded when he heard the Aussie accent. His face clouded over. "We've been told about you and we're not to show you anything in the gym," he confided. "The guy who let you in has been suspended."

Meg took over, as usual in such situations. Oozing charm, she explained that we were looking to open an Australian franchise of the American brand. Bullshit again.

"I wouldn't do that," Chuck blurted out. "I'm really struggling. Can't make ends meet." Encouraged by Meg, Chuck let it all hang out. Seems the local council would not give Chuck a 24-hour licence, so he had to operate on restricted hours. His premises were also too cramped, even for small-box, and tucked away, without adequate signage. He was very unhappy with the franchisor; and when Meg sympathised, he proceeded to tell us all that was wrong with the model: royalties too high, no franchisee support... the list went on.

We also didn't know at the time that the biggest American 24-hour gym operator, Anytime Fitness, had just given the Australian franchise rights to three members of my former round table (more about that later).

That night I booked a seedy Pasadena motel; it was all I could afford. The heat was stifling, even for Spring, and we sat on falling-apart banana lounges beside a green, bacteria-ridden concrete pool, knowing any attempt to cool off could endanger our lives.

We didn't care. As we toasted each other with Budweisers, I looked at Meg and said: "I've got to do this back home, regardless, you know."

"I'm with you, Bobby," she said. As optimism and hope replaced pessimism and despair, the Pasadena motel suddenly looked like a five-star resort.

Next day, heading down the LA freeway to the airport, I mused out loud, "What are we going to call the new gyms?" We tossed around several names without success.

"Gotta be short, sharp and sexy," I said. I hated all the gym names I knew of. They were always FitGym or BodyMove – terrible generic monsters with no passion or soul.

Frustrated at our lack of progress, I again thought aloud: "What are they going to do with their key when they go in the door after hours?"

Put the key in the lock, said Meg. Turn the key. "What about 'Turnkey Gyms'?" she tried.

Too much like turkey.

Suddenly, with the famous Hollywood sign looking down from the hills behind, it was as if all tinsel town's long-dead matinee idols, gazing down benignly on an ageing fitness entrepreneur who should

ZAP! They're going to zap the key on the pad. Zap it. I felt like I'd just discovered the secret recipe for KFC chicken.

be retired and home with his Milo and slippers, decided to grant him one last bolt of blockbuster inspiration.

The bolt hit my brain like a pinball machine. Too frightened to speak loudly in case anybody else heard us above the roar of the freeway, I whispered in my best American slang: "I got it. I got it. Dude, I've got it."

"ZAP! They're going to zap the key on the pad. Zap it." I felt like I'd just discovered Colonel Sanders' secret recipe for KFC chicken.

Now we screamed into the LA smog, casting off the blanket that had been smothering our brains: ZAP, ZAP, ZAP. Yes, ZAP. That nailed it, and we knew it.

We bellowed ZAP deliriously for several minutes until it threatened to wake up every resident in Beverly Hills and Bel Air – and even Mulholland Drive. I'm sure everyone heard us.

The cramped, sleepless trip home went unnoticed. Mission accomplished: we had an idea, we had a name. Now all we needed was a business.

Rapid-Fire Robert furiously worked on the figures over lots of cheap Qantas reds and plastic food. I couldn't believe the end result. If my numbers were correct, we could make a 30 to 35 per cent return on minimal investment.

Goodbye Club Silly Wanker. We were off on an adventure bigger than *Ben-Hur, Star Wars* and *Jurassic Park* combined.

Sorry, Randy – just hope you got your membership back.

IF IT WAS EASY, EVERYBODY WOULD BE DOING IT

The world is full of people with talent who come up with great ideas, but very few turn their ideas into a successful business. Dreaming is easy. It's the risk-taking and hard work that follow that count.

How many times have your friends heard you say, with great indignation when reading about yet another success story: "I thought of that years ago I was just too busy at the time to do anything about it"?

Yeah right. What you really mean is that you lacked confidence, were too lazy to get out of your comfort zone, or too frightened to take a risk. Or all of those. Don't worry, you're not alone. Unfortunately, most people are like that. That's why there are winners and losers in this world. And, what's more, unless you change now, you'll be wandering

Please, please don't let the world dictate to you. You dictate to the world, take it by the scruff of the neck and tell it what you are going to do.

around in old age as an if-only-er, full of regrets, saying things like, "I'm always unlucky" or "Wasn't meant to be."

Please, please, don't let the world dictate to you. You dictate to the world, take it by the scruff of the neck and tell it what you are going to do. You must be focused and single-minded. Nothing should stand in your way. Most people are successful once they know exactly what they want to achieve. The problem is, the majority can't decide.

Turn into a benevolent dictator... and be sparing with the benevolence. You can't start a successful new business by committee, board of directors or focus groups. The old saying that a camel is a horse designed by a committee is so often borne out. The innovator has to be you, and you alone.

Relentlessly drive the early stages, then the adrenalin will flow – you will cross the Rubicon and burn the bridge behind you; there will be no turning back. Sixty-hour weeks will become the norm. I love that feeling, despite the trepidation. And I'm urging you to feel the same way. Challenges are what life's all about.

But before you rush in and quit your existing job to start a new business, try to at least do the groundwork while retaining income as an employee. It's called moonlighting. As an employer I'm uncomfortable saying this, but you're a fool if you don't attempt to use your existing infrastructure to at least get things started.

I did. While working as a subeditor at *The Mercury* newspaper in the early 1980s, I started an indoor cricket centre and, yes, worked the phones to do the preliminary planning. My newspaper hours were from 4pm to about midnight. After the centre opened I used to work shifts there from 8am to 3pm and then go straight to my *Mercury* job.

I was editor of the *Sunday Tasmanian* when I resurrected the Lifestyle gym as Dockside – and, although it was a more senior position and required fifty hours a week, I still managed to do the groundwork while keeping my job. I even had employees bring up the Dockside cheques for me to sign during newspaper hours – on the pretext of job interviews. My workmates used to stir me and say I was running my gym business from Rupert Murdoch's office – they even started calling me Rupert – but it was a means to an end. When Dockside officially opened, I resigned and became a full-time managing director. Sorry, Rupert, but I suspect you would've done the same. And I still put in more than I got out; including from 9am Saturday to 2am Sunday, when the first paper came off the press (that's seventeen hours straight).

People make a choice about leisure time, and I respect that. But if you want to knock off at 5pm each day and not work weekends, business is not for you. I don't think I've ever worked fewer than sixty hours a week; and, together with my wife, Steph, I still raised a family.

With Zap, there was no question of moonlighting. I was already in the fitness industry full-time, whether I liked it or not.

As part of my personal life goals, I always imagine that I'm in a time capsule and I fire it forward ten years. OK, it's now 2031... what am I going to regret not having done? I did this exercise when I went into politics, and even though it didn't work out the way I wanted (heck, I did become leader of the Liberal Party), I'm so glad I tried because otherwise I would've been walking around saying: "I should've gone into politics and I would've been Premier by now and I could've done all these great things for Tassie." Well, I didn't become Premier – and didn't deserve to – but at least I had a crack. No regrets now. Not ever.

So, back in 2008 I climbed into the projection machine again and fired myself forward to 2018. What would I regret? Not starting 24-hour gyms, that's what.

I arrived back from my whirlwind US fact-finding mission to the usual complaints from Club Silly Wanker members: "Where have you been? On holiday in America. You must be making plenty of money. Knew I was being charged too much."

But there was also mutiny in the air. The spa pump had broken down and the spa was closed. The only happy person was the banana in pyjamas upstairs; a receptionist hadn't turned up for work the previous morning and our scantily clad members had to wait in the freezing cold Hobart air until help arrived.

The grizzling and moaning wafted around me like a junk-food addict's fart. I didn't care any more. All I could think of was Zap. This was my salvation: I had a way out.

Suddenly my spirits – usually suppressed by the negativity of Club Silly Wanker – rose. Now to get started. I knew it wouldn't be easy. If it was easy, everybody would be doing it.

DON'T GET RIPPED OFF BY FRANCHISES

A ll the 24-hour clubs we saw in the United States operated as franchises. But I don't like franchises.

Yes, I know the arguments: it's the quickest way to expand – using someone else's money – if you're the founder. It also cuts down the risk. And the franchisee finds the site, saving a lot of travel and time. But for the poor old franchisee – who's legally stitched up like a Bangladesh garment factory worker – it's a different story. They are told what to do and there's hell to pay if they don't obey. The franchisor calls all the shots. Then there's the added costs, which are usually outlandish, with big margins added to everything – territory rights, equipment, fit-out, bloated royalties, marketing, and (in the case of gyms) direct debits.

Avoid them. Do it yourself.

I've always had a strong independent streak – sometimes to my detriment. As a boarder at Launceston Grammar School in the 1950s, when authority was brutal (5am cold showers daily, and six cuts to the backside with a willow cane if you misbehaved), I refused to conform. That's probably why I left school after failing Form 4 (now Year 10). And in politics I couldn't hack the party system and the rigidity it placed on members. I should never have joined the Liberal Party – let alone become its leader. My rightful place in parliament would have been as an independent.

Australian fitness operators are obsessed with buying master franchises from the United States – Anytime Fitness, Snap Fitness, Orange Theory, Crunch Fitness, Planet Fitness, CrossFit, to name a few. They all originated in America. But while Australia's biggest chains – Fitness First and Goodlife – were copied, they were not franchised. Goodlife is a massive Canadian chain. Fitness First originated in England and was British owned when it came to Australia in the 1990s.

A well-known group of Australian gym owners procured the Anytime franchise rights for Australia from the US founder and then franchised around the country, paying a royalty to their peers in the United States – but also charging huge fees to the Aussies who bought in. The group did very well, because they got in early, as did some of their early franchisees. But they were using another entrepreneur's product – and I could never understand why they didn't do it themselves and avoid being known as an American imitator. Sure, I admit, Zap knocked off some ideas from California, but we formed our own brand, did it a different way and fully owned all our gyms.

Back to 2008. Knowing the Anytime franchise was being brought to Australia meant there was no time to waste. I contacted my long-standing equipment supplier in Melbourne, Life Fitness, to choose the gear I wanted for my first 24-hour gym.

"Great idea," said managing director Paul McClure, son of the founder, Robert. "You can do at least four Anytime franchises in

Hobart. I can contact the Anytime owners to let them know. They're in Minneapolis at the moment tying up the deal."

"I'm doing it myself, Paul," I cautioned. "I hate franchises."

There was a stunned silence. "[24-hour gyms] are not easy to set up... You need security and systems, and starting from scratch will put you way behind," Paul continued. "And then there's the competition when Anytime comes to Hobart..." By the time he had finished, I had stopped listening.

If you're a true entrepreneur, you just want to do it yourself. I would hate to be subservient to a master; there's pride and satisfaction in building your own brand and, hopefully, seeing it grow and succeed. And let's face it, you either worry about staff or worry about franchisees – it's one or the other. I'd prefer staff. And you keep better control over quality and replication, which is what I was about.

I must confess that, later, as Zap began to grow interstate, I again considered franchising, despite my prejudice. It was becoming difficult to manage company-owned gyms in diverse locations. For instance, if you wanted to open a gym in Adelaide, there was an advantage in having a franchisee rather than constant interstate trips to oversee the setting up, opening, and ongoing management.

I contacted a franchising consultancy firm to explore the possibilities. They claimed to have been involved in franchises such as Boost Juice. For a hefty fee, about $20,000, three key executives flew to Hobart to see whether Zap was "franchise ready". We met at the Salamanca Inn across the road from Club Silly Wanker, which was still limping along and losing money. The "meeting" consisted of going over old ground on sheets of butchers' paper. Then followed a session in Melbourne, where one of the key people fell asleep halfway through. He woke up rubbing his eyes, wondering where he was. Fantasyland, I concluded – the same place as us if we continued with this outfit. He blamed one of his kids for keeping him up all night with toothache.

To avoid such pain for Zap, I pulled out and refused to pay the bill. Legal threats followed, which I ignored.

Don't buy franchises unless you're desperate. Do it yourself; that's much more satisfying.

The other advantage of not franchising – and owning all the gyms yourself – is that, if you want to sell in the future, what you are offering is much more attractive to a potential purchaser.

Buyers don't have to worry about temperamental franchisees creating problems. If the gyms are all owned by one person, or company, it's much cleaner and easier. We were to find this out first hand many years later.

Don't buy franchises unless you're desperate. Do it yourself; that's much more satisfying. And if you're starting a business, don't take the easy way out and franchise too early. If you're short on funds, borrow – and hold on...

BEWARE OF BUSINESS PARTNERS

I f you want to fall out with family and friends, I know of a sure-fire method: Go into business with them. There are exceptions, but mostly it never works. You'd probably be better off saying: "I hate your guts and I don't want to speak to you again, so let's go into business to seal the deal."

My biggest mistake in business has been to have too many partners. Only one has never let me down; most have cost me lots of time, energy and money. I know it's difficult initially, but my advice is to keep as much of the business as you can – for as long as you can.

When I arrived back from the United States, I hit the ground running. My first step was to register the business name ZAP under Robert Reginald Cheek. This was my idea – and for the first time in my life I

My biggest mistake in business has been to have too many partners.

wouldn't have business partners. It seemed that I always came up with the ideas, took most of the initial risks, did all the hard work – and then either through ignorance or necessity gave away equity to people who really didn't deserve it. And invariably they conveyed their gratitude and thanks by dudding me at the end.

In the early days I was forced to take on partners because I didn't have much money and was advised to share the liability in any high-risk venture. But I still gave away too much – more than I needed to. It's a sorry litany and a warning to all budding entrepreneurs.

Here are my four biggest errors.

Mistake one: My first serious venture (apart from the Lifestyle dalliance) was in the early 1980s, when I realised I would never earn enough on a journalist's wage – much as I loved the job – to send my kids to private schools and do all the other things on my list of goals.

With my sporting background and love of all things requiring physical exertion, I teamed up with another subeditor, Dale Brakey, a Burnie boy who had recently returned from Perth to work at The Mockery – as it was fondly known. He too was ambitious, but he had even less money than I, which meant he was nearly broke.

Working together in the sub-editors' room from 4pm to midnight, we had plenty of time during the day to hatch our lofty plans. Brakey and I decided to develop a squash centre on Hobart's Eastern Shore and we agreed to an equal partnership: 50–50. Long drunken discussions ensued at nearby Maloney's Hotel during the notorious subeditors' pub breaks. It was an era when newspapers encouraged drinking on the job as a means to gain dubious stories from other drunks. After an hour's break at Maloney's – which usually meant sculling eight or ten beers – we would return and produce the front pages of the next day's paper.

Through an old Clarence footy mate and real estate agent, David Anderson, I found the perfect site in Percy Street, Bellerive. It was formerly a rubbish tip and had old cars and god knows what else buried beneath the surface – enough to make the owner, Clarence City Council, and other potential buyers write it off because of the building difficulties.

The late architect Alex Kostromin solved the problem by designing a lightweight building on a floating slab. The council couldn't believe its luck when some idiot came in offering to buy their former rubbish tip. I paid the $3,000 deposit – all I could come up with – on my credit card, with the remaining $100,000 to be paid in twenty-four months. I was gambling on generating enough cash from the business by then to repay the balance. Council was just glad to get rid of it.

Not sure if it was inspired by Maloney's, but our squash courts morphed into a roller-skating rink and then a swim centre as we battled to come up with a viable proposition. Fortuitously, a mate returned from Perth and mentioned a new game taking off in the West called indoor cricket. We checked it out and, with the recklessness of youth, decided this was it.

Bank lenders thought I was mad: "So, you want us to lend you money to play a new game that no one's heard of in a building that's not there yet," the incredulous Commonwealth Bank manager scoffed as he showed me out the door. "Sorry, no. Buy a newsagency instead." No thanks, I had already done that.

Finally, the old Savings Bank of Tasmania (SBT) came to the party. After three years of battling to get the venture off the ground, going to hell and back, working fifteen-hour days, and putting the family home on the line, I thought we were finally able to proceed.

Wrong. Brakey decided to throw in his lot with a franchised operation in Western Australia. He took a 15 per cent share in the rival group and built an opposition indoor cricket centre in Moonah. Ironically, I read about it in *The Mercury*.

Brakey and his new partners tried to develop a rival centre not far from my Bellerive site. Luckily, I knew a resident in the street, Roger Viney, who helped collect a petition in the area and we stopped the project.

I grimly fought on and got the job done. Thanks, partner.

Mistake two: My gamble paid off and the Eastern Shore Indoor Cricket Centre was hugely successful. But I believed I had to bring well-known sportsmen into the indoor cricket venture to help promote the product. So I offered shares to a group of Tasmanian cricketers – one an ex-Test player – at the same entry price as myself. I should've just employed them; the business didn't need big names anyway.

Tensions developed within the group, so in the early 1990s I decided to sell out and do something else. We agreed on a fair price – shook hands – and I signed the contract in good faith and left on an overseas trip with my family. The partners repaid my generosity by coming up with an imaginary extra debt they claimed I owed – and they wouldn't countersign until I reduced the price.

My trip – along with faith in others – was ruined.

Thanks, partners.

Footnote: Perhaps Karma does exist. After I left the business, they made an ill-advised overseas investment and had to sell the centre to pay their debts.

Mistake three: I formed a syndicate to buy the Dockside gym Hunter Street building but made the error of including two outsiders who didn't have a share in the operating business. Stupid. The outsiders wanted inflated rent for the building to maximise their return – and the operators just wanted – well, a fair deal. Continual tension and in-fighting.

Thanks, partners.

Mistake four: In the meantime, I'd helped one of the Eastern Shore cricketers become a Dockside shareholder and part of the building syndicate. When he had to stump up extra cash to develop apartments, he refused – even though he had the assets – and threatened to go bankrupt if we forced the issue. We had to cover his losses out of our own pockets.

Thanks, partner.

So, this time there'd be no "Thanks, partners". This was my baby. I'd learned my lessons the hard way. Now I would fail or succeed on my own terms.

Or so I thought. It was 2008 and the GFC had hit hard. All I wanted to do was lease some equipment and have enough funds for the fit-out. Confidently I got in touch with the National Australia Bank (NAB) where we had our leasing for Club Silly Wanker. We'd never missed a monthly payment. The manager was a personal friend.

"Mate, thinking about doing a new gym, just want to lease some more equipment, give you some more business, mate. We must have lunch again soon."

He said he'd get back to me. I waited. The call eventually came several weeks later, and it ended any future lunches.

"Sorry, Bob, can't do it. The bank has a ban on all gym equipment."

An interstate cowboy gym chain named Beach House had gone bust. I knew they were cowboys because they had wanted to buy Club Silly Wanker – that's how desperate they were. (I would've sold, but they wanted me to leave most of the purchase price in the business and pay out of profits. Great idea, especially when it was making a loss.)

The surprise was the stupidity of the banks. Both the Commonwealth Bank (CBA) and NAB had taken leases on Beach House's second-hand gym equipment at inflated values and had lost millions. And now the rest of us had to suffer for their incompetence.

The CBA gave the same answer as NAB: "It's now national policy." I had banked with them since my schoolboy elephant money-box days, but there was no sentiment during the GFC. I exploded and told the manager that they should make decisions based on individuals and not punish us because of Beach House, then hung up.

A few days later the CBA manager, Michael Goss, rang me: "We can't do it for you individually, it's too risky, but if you want to use the same company structure you've got for Club Salamanca [which included the heavily mortgaged building] we might be able to get it over the line."

Shit, shit, shit. Here we go again. Still bloody partners. I owned 55 per cent of the Silly Wanker and the other 45 per cent belonged to two other shareholders. One was good and always supportive, the other unpredictable. Although at least I had control. I desperately tried to get the money from other sources, but in the end it was the status quo or nothing.

I badly wanted to do Zap; I felt it was my destiny. Do I go ahead with 55 per cent, or risk doing nothing? Of course, it was go ahead. I wanted it too much. The business name and accounts were in my name. They and the Zap brand and logo remained so. Eventually, I leased them back to the company. Right to the end, direct debits on members' bank accounts and credit card statements appeared as "RR Cheek trading as Zap Fitness". I wish.

The decision by the CBA would end up costing me lots of money and heaps of unnecessary heartache. But at least Zap was ready to zap the world.

MAKE DEAD INSECTS FLY

We had a name but no logo. It was critical to rectify this – because branding either makes or breaks a business. I always saw the Zap logo as being like the comic book superheroes of my childhood: you know, ZAP, POW, BAM!... as in some fight with punches being thrown, and maybe a lightning bolt somewhere. Stupid in hindsight.

A local part-time graphic designer was recruited to come up with the logo. But first I had a new shareholder problem – or to be more exact, the spouse of one of the partners, who claimed to have a PhD in marketing. Whoopee. (Sorry, but I have no time for university degrees in marketing, advertising or any other subjective discipline.)

One morning I was folding towels in Club Silly Wanker when our front-desk receptionist presented me with an "urgent" letter from one of my two shareholders.

HEY!...HEY, YOU WITH THE GENERIC, HOMOGENISED NAMES...BUZZ OFF!
zap
Fitness 24/7

I was speechless. All the homogenised names I detested, and my beloved Zap a "dead insect".

Dated 25/07/08, it was signed by the shareholder but contained urgent advice from his marketing guru:

"Bob, for your consideration – ideas for brand name:

Energise

Exercise Anytime

Feel Fit

"Zap – sounds like a dead insect."

I was speechless. All the homogenised names I detested, and my beloved Zap a "dead insect". And this from a so-called marketing expert! I imagined a fly lying on its back, wings and legs thrashing in its spray-induced death throes – my gym reduced to a blowfly.

Of course, I ignored the illogical advice and told the shareholder to, basically, go bite his bum. Stay out of it; I'm the majority shareholder and CEO, so I'll do what I want. Just shut up and I'll make you some money.

There was indignation and *harrumphs* from the source but my other partner, as always, supported my view. Thank goodness I didn't deviate from my plan, otherwise we may have ended up being called "Feel Fit". I imagined McDonald's being named "Fast Burgers"; or Apple "Computer World"; or Starbucks "Coffee House". Branding and naming are so important. Always go for something different that will stand out – even better if it's one word and ideally one syllable.

Nevertheless, the antagonists didn't give up. They had one more try. Apart from being a "dead fly", Zap was in the last quartile of the alphabet and the PhD theses said that definitely wouldn't work. Really? Bet Virgin, Woolworths and Xerox would've changed their names if they'd known that.

Normally, I file such nonsense in the rubbish bin but, thinking it might become an historic note, or something to laugh at when Zap ruled the world – or at least Tasmania – I kept the letter. Now it sits framed on my wall alongside the spray tan memento, with the inscription: "Dead insects really can fly." Proof yet again that, when it comes to business, postgraduate publications are no replacement for the School-of-Hard-Knocks one pager, dot-point number one: "Stick to your guns."

The graphic artist came back with his logo. It was wedge-shaped with a lightning bolt – but sadly in orange and black – the standard budget colours of cut-price airline Jetstar. We intended our fees to be cheap, but not for our service to be lacking. I wanted Zap gyms to be bold and brassy – no cringe-worthy colours or lack of signage.

Meg and I drove around the streets of Hobart in the dead of winter – no better place to see which colours stood out through the drizzle – and we decided the choice had to be red. After all, there's a reason McDonald's and most fast-food joints are mainly that colour.

So, red and white with a slight touch of yellow it was to be. Our artist was unimpressed – as most advertising types are if you don't like their work – but agreed to go back to his drawing board. He withdrew his services soon after. But not before recommending another graphic artist, Nathanael Jeanneret.

The name was certainly impressive. After lots of discussion Nathanael came up with our much-loved logo – no dead insects or can of Mortein included – just a distinctive red wedge with the Zap name in white, plus a touch of Macca's yellow around the P to give that "kapow" look.

Now, I will admit that using a name like Zap means you have to let people know what the hell it is, so we elongated the tail of the "p" to include the words "fitness 24/7". And for good measure we made our slogan "work out day and night". This was important because, don't forget, no one knew what a 24-hour gym was in 2008.

Later, I mentioned to Nathanael that it was a masterstroke putting the yellow "kapow" marks around the "p" of Zap. He looked at me strangely. "They were supposed to represent the minutes of a clock to signify 24 hours," he said. Kapow! It still worked beautifully.

The other masterstroke was to plaster our web address all over the fronts of our gyms. We wanted to direct people to our website so we could explain in more detail what we were about. These days this is de rigueur, but back then it was innovative.

The dead fly was about to take off.

WINSTON CHURCHILL AND THE FREAK FACTORY

On 20 August 1940, at the height of the Battle of Britain, the United Kingdom's great wartime prime minister, Winston Churchill, famously said, "Never... was so much owed by so many to so few." He was referring to the brave British Spitfire pilots who fought off the German invasion.

Little did Churchill know that, seventy years later, his declaration would also apply to the Battle of Zap. I could have added the words *dickheads* and idiots to the "so many" – but, out of deference to Winston, I demurred. I'll explain later.

Club Silly Wanker was already doing business with a crowd called Alpha Audio (nothing to do with today's business by the same name in Melbourne). It was run by Tim McCulloch, who'd also been president of the local Lindisfarne branch of the Liberal Party when I was in politics. Bearded, affable Tim installed cardio theatre (treadmills individually hooked up to sound and TV) at Club Silly Wanker, and I knew he also had links to security technicians. With our penchant for nicknames, and his whiskers, we initially christened him Rolf – after Rolf Harris – but we hastily changed that to the Ned of Ned Kelly after the disgraced entertainer's demise. Ned suited Tim.

I got on well with Ned and his offsider, Anders. Ned operated from premises in Smith Street, North Hobart. In a light-hearted moment I named it the Freak Factory. The place was full of sinister machines, wires, cables and racks better utilised as props for a horror movie; I fully expected Dracula to materialise out of the smoke-filled, beer-stained interior. Every Friday night, all Ned's cohorts and hangers-on gathered over a few VBs to discuss the latest offerings of their enterprise, which included the unworldly and weird. It was like grown-up Halloween.

Ned listened open-mouthed when I outlined my plans for 24-hour fitness clubs. "We're going to open 24 hours and we need a security system and point-of-sale mechanism that works with the zap of a key," I said. "Also, it needs to be hooked up to our direct debit system."

He didn't hesitate. "Got just the man for you."

Into our lives lurched a gangling 195 centimetre (6 foot, 4 inches) laconic, chain-smoking Telstra employee, whom we christened Dr Strangelove after the famous character played by Peter Sellars in the 1960s movie of that name. A more anti-fitness, anti-everything kind of guy could never have been imagined, let alone invented. Little did we know what a profound effect he would have on our lives and business over the next ten years.

"How can you come up with a 24/7 gym system when you still work for Telstra?" was the first question I put to Dr Strangelove.

"Because they have so many staff they don't know who works for them," he drawled in the under-stated monotone I would come to know so well.

"What do you know about fitness?" I demanded.

"Nothing, I hate it," he replied, exhaling smoke. "Just show me your present gym system and I'll work it out."

Dr Strangelove turned up in his Telstra work gear – white open-necked shirt and baggy dark suit with an oversize belt dangling down his leg like an exposed penis. Smelling of Camel cigarettes and beer, he sprawled out next to our fit, tanned, health-conscious and now very apprehensive Club Silly Wanker receptionist while she showed him our up-market, full-service system. This bloke is never going to make it, I worried.

After a few hours sussing out our current system, Dr Strangelove got up to leave. "Can't work it out?" I asked.

"Leave it with me and I'll get back to you in a few days," was his reply. Last I'll hear of him, I thought.

A few days later, Strangelove called. "Piece of piss," he said. "I'll have it up and running in a few weeks."

Strangelove, working day and night in the Freak Factory, had cobbled together bits and pieces from every online system he could legally – and possibly not – get his hands on. But the end result was a brilliant, elaborate, unique system. Trouble was, it was also fatally flawed. The entire set-up depended on one man to operate it, and one company to supply all the entrance keys. In other words, Strangelove and his fellow Freak Factory aficionados had me hung upside down from the highest crossbar with dumbbells tied tightly around my scrotum. How they must have laughed into the night over those VBs as they thought about the technology luddite they were doing business with.

Most 24-hour gym systems are in two parts: the point of sale; and a separate elaborate security section with cameras positioned over the entry door to catch any member letting in strangers (as happened in

San Diego) or otherwise doing the wrong thing. Multiple cameras are spread around the gym interior as well.

Strangelove's system was different. He integrated point of sale and security so it couldn't be separated. When the key zapped and the door opened, the person entering was photographed and the image could be called up to check with the original membership photo if required. Many times the person entering was a teenaged, tattooed lad, but his photo showed a middle-aged woman.

Sounds good? In practice, we would discover in the days ahead that the photo depended on the door opening in normal fashion – and suitable light. Often we'd get a half-opened door or the back of someone's head. And sometimes, especially in bright sunlight, we'd get a yellow haze. Would-be gatecrashers took to wearing hoodies and beanies pulled down over their eyes to avoid detection.

Staff were instructed to check the overnight entries as soon as they started work at 10am every day – and to ring any member suspected of foul play and threaten them with suspension. Mostly it was guesswork, and members became irate if they were falsely accused of wrongdoing. But as a deterrent it was very successful, and that was the aim. So although the system was far from perfect, it would be good enough to get us started.

Each gym would have its own hardware setup and operated independently, but the "brain" of the business was installed at our first gym, in the Hobart suburb of Rosny. It contained all our data and, if it had been broken into and damaged, it could have brought down the whole caboodle, every gym in the chain.

We were also unique in that we did all our own direct debits in-house. All franchised gyms outsourced this facility to third parties (and the franchisor made a fortune by charging the unsuspecting franchisees a margin over the normal fee). In other words, our systems were homemade, fragile, dependent on one person, and could fail at any time, bringing our business down with them. I didn't realise this until much later.

Cost-wise Strangelove's system seemed like a steal: only $12,000 for the whole thing. But he never wrote a code or documented the information. If we fell out, or he was sick, I was lost – and so was the Zap business. And he knew it. Strangelove would often threaten to withdraw his services – and one time he did walk out. As it happened, we developed system problems at the time. Desperately, I rang his colleagues trying to seek solutions, but all they could say was, "He has it all in his head."

The initial charge might have been cheap... but Strangelove hastily incorporated his own business and tried to make it a fifteen-year lease, with him retaining ownership of the intellectual property. Luckily, before he began work I had put in writing that I was to own the system, and after months of haggling he finally gave me outright ownership for another measly $1,000. Cheap – and nasty. But workable.

The Zapper keys – as we called them, attempting to make out they were something special because we charged $69.90 for a key that could be bought for a few cents direct from China – were programmed at the Freak Factory. And, of course, they were coded in such a way that it was very hard to replicate them. So, we were charged more, and we could only get them from Ned's factory. Therefore the Freak Factory could also bring down our business, by withholding the supply of keys for our members. And one day they attempted to do just that.

I rang up for more keys and was told by an employee I hadn't paid an account so couldn't have any. The claim was false, and we didn't have enough keys to last the day. In a fit of rage, I jumped in my car and roared up to Smith Street, double-parking with a screech of the brakes. I savagely crashed open the front door and demanded keys from one of Ned's contractors.

"Tim says you're not getting any until you've paid your bills," he said smugly.

This little upstart was threatening the viability of my business. I picked him up by the bib of his overalls and, hoisting him to just a few centimetres from my face, snapped menacingly, "Just give me

Make sure you have plenty of people who know how to operate your systems.

my bloody keys that I've paid for." I was hoping the contractor was a pacifist and my bluster would work.

At that moment, luckily for both of us, his wife, who also worked at the factory, heard the commotion and rushed out screaming, "They're in the cupboard," and shoved a large box of keys into my arms. I skedaddled out of there before the police could be called.

What a way to do business. I immediately changed the key contract to another supplier – who was unfortunately still connected to the Freak Factory cartel – and the arrangement was better, but still suspect. Try as I might, I could never replicate the keys myself. And so, we were always operating under the threat of being brought down by a lousy Zapper – or lack thereof.

As the Zap business grew bigger, I also tried to outsource our systems and direct debits to a third party. But Strangelove had done his job well. The outsourcers were baffled by the booby-trap system; it was going to cost millions to change over. I'm not saying Strangelove deliberately built the system so he became indispensable, but that was the result.

Desperate, I employed Melbourne software consultants to give an independent risk assessment of our situation. Like all consultancies, it was a waste of money. They told me what I already knew: If Dr Strangelove leaves, your business could fail. Stroke of genius. Thanks.

Eventually I employed more programmers and network operators to stop the reliance on Strangelove. But like all computer nerds, he still managed to keep control over the staff and his systems – until he had health issues and resigned when I needed him most (more of that later).

Don't rely on the likes of Winston Churchill's "few". Make sure you have plenty of people who know how to operate your systems; and make sure you have the source code fully documented.

You might start small, but, as you grow, your business can be held to ransom, just as ours was.

DON'T GET OFF YOUR BIKE – KEEP PEDALLING

'm ashamed to admit this, but I'd better get it off my chest in this chapter because it leads to one of my life's great guiding principles.

When I was a kid growing up in Evandale, a small country town about 20 kilometres from Launceston in northern Tasmania, I would become frustrated and lose my temper if things didn't go my way, which was often. And I was a shocking sport. I'd let tantrums and temperament (smashing racquets and bats) get in the way of harnessing my natural skill and ability.

I always made Bradman-like scores when playing cricket with the mostly dirt-poor township kids in the back paddock because, as the wealthy farmer's son, I owned the bat, ball and wickets. The other kids knew only too well that to get me out meant the end of the game. So every ball was tossed short of a length, well wide of the stumps on the home-made grass pitch; this would ensure my survival, until I notched an inevitable century and retired to great applause undefeated.

And during the footy season, I nominated myself as umpire as well as captain in our "pick-up" matches, making sure I received loads of controversial free kicks 10 metres from goal dead in front at critical moments in "time on". There was never any dissent from the town kids – otherwise they wouldn't have had a football.

In tennis, during epic contests against my sister's boyfriend, Graham – who eventually became my brother-in-law – on our family's cracked cement court (Dad had insisted on building it himself but the slabs lifted soon after, leaving giant ridges), I'd call urgent toilet breaks if I was behind in the deciding set. On the only occasion when the benign and much older Graham, no doubt not wanting to risk losing my sister by giving me a good smack around the ears, looked like winning, I stormed off and smashed my racquet on the net post.

Yes, I was a disgrace and deserved a good thrashing, but I was lucky to have a genial and kind-hearted Dad, who believed sparing the rod and spoiling the child was the best philosophy. According to my sister, Janice, the only time Dad ever belted me – in the family's only bathroom – he came out crying because of what he'd had to do. Dad's patience gave me far more than any whipping: two pieces of wisdom that have shaped my life.

The first – after one of my inevitable dummy spits – was the admission that he, too, had a terrible temper as a child – until one day an old farmhand took him aside and whispered in his ear, "Only cowards lose their temper." In the battle-hardened, derring-do days of the early twentieth century Dad didn't want to be branded a coward, and he never lost his temper again.

Although I tried hard to replicate Dad's temper epiphany, and certainly improved in this regard, things such as staff not turning up for work, or governments getting in the way of business, or excessive red tape impeding progress, often lit my fuse. Until I looked up to the heavens and said, "Sorry, Dad."

Dad's second major contribution, after one particularly bad explosion, still guides my life, and always will. He put his arm around me, locked his soft blue eyes onto my tear-stained cheeks and said in his calm, reassuring manner, "Don't get off your bike, son. Keep pedalling."

Don't get off your bike, keep pedalling. When life gets tough don't give up, just keep on going. I've always remembered those words, and they've provided great comfort and inspiration in times of worry and stress. Thanks, Dad. Your wisdom and patience in an era when every parent believed in iron discipline and corporal punishment made me a much better person and better equipped to face the world. And I certainly needed to "keep pedalling" when I embarked on finding a site for our first Zap gym.

I knew Tasmania well. My great-grandparents emigrated from the English county of Essex in 1855, meaning my family went back a long way; and I'd lived and played football in all regions of the state. Sitting down with a large map and red pins, I earmarked potential sites in Tassie's three main population areas: nine in the south, four in the north and two on the north-west coast.

Tassie, with its 2008 population of around 500,000 split evenly between the north and south, was the most decentralised state in Australia – and it still is. Hobart, the capital, had an approximate population of just 200,000 (unlike the mainland capitals, which dominate their states) which is why there's so much parochialism and rivalry between areas. It also had the unenviable reputation as the most obese part of the Australian continent.

As well as aiming to build a successful business and make money for my retirement, I wanted to take fitness to the masses, and provide affordable, accessible gyms for everyone. I used the line that I wanted

An old farmhand took Dad aside and whispered in his ear, "Only cowards lose their temper."

Zap gyms on every street corner: an exaggeration, but it adequately summed up my sentiments.

My lofty ambition of fifteen gyms was met with disbelief in some quarters. But I wanted to emulate other Tassie businesses I admired that had built a statewide brand, such as Banjo's bakeries (although most were franchised); Chickenfeed discount stores (owned by my great friend the late Rudi Sypkes and his brother, Peter, before they were sold); and Video City (whose days were numbered). Due to my statewide ambitions, the plan was to employ one firm to find all the sites and negotiate the rental deals, with a success fee attached. I decided on Hobart property consultants and valuers Brothers Newton. I'd been good friends with Charles Brothers, one of the original partners, who had since moved on.

The initial meeting was productive enough, but when the other principal, Scott Newton, became involved my plans were treated with great scepticism and suspicion, especially the unknown quantity of 24-hour-gyms; and, heavens above, fifteen of the things! It felt like the indoor cricket centre all over again. Eventually, we agreed on expenses for each site and a success fee of $6,000 for each lease contract signed. I left the meeting with the promise that I would be kept updated on progress. And so, feeling all was in hand, I proceeded to work on the operational side of the gyms.

After about a month and no contact from Brothers Newton, I became concerned and phoned them.

"How many sites have you nailed down?" I said.

Silence. Could I come in for a "progress" meeting?

Scepticism had given way to procrastination. Unbelievably, they had no sites. One month's "progress" amounted to writing letters to real estate agents in each area I had identified, then sitting back and waiting for a reply. "I could've done that," I protested. "Can't you be more proactive?" The answer was "no" and we parted company shortly after – by that time, six weeks wasted, with no result. I decided to take matters into my own hands and get the sites myself, one by one.

I called a former suburban bank manager, Rod Cohen, a good bloke who had recently gone into commercial real estate, and asked if he knew of any sites suitable for a gym (without saying what sort of gym) on my old stamping ground of Hobart's Eastern Shore.

"Get back to you, mate," he said.

Here we go again, I thought. But no, Rod called the next day. He had two potential sites around the Eastlands Shopping Centre at Rosny, one of my preferred areas. One was an office block, the other a Blockbuster video store that the owner wanted to close.

And so started my love affair with video stores. Who would've thought, in the 1980s, that video stores would close and be replaced by gyms about twenty years later? It's almost as though the early video store owners thought, "Ah, well, if videos go out of fashion, we can always open a gym."

The stores were open plan – no office walls or partitions, about the right size for a small-box gym, and usually well located. The Blockbuster store was no exception, a ripping site of about 360 square metres in a separate block of downmarket retail stores just off the Eastlands car park. My co-tenants included Centrelink, Vinnies and Cash Converters. Privately, I joked that if 24-hour gyms didn't work I'd be first in line for Centrelink dole payments, could buy cheap clothes from Vinnies and could cash in the gym equipment at Cash Converters. But great site that it was, the original video store still presented plenty of problems. First it was still operating; second, the owner was absent;

and third, I didn't want to start paying rent until I had received planning approvals for a 24-hour gym. This would take time.

Luckily, I knew the landlord, my former accountant and good friend, Carl Rooke. This obviously gave me a distinct advantage. With Rod by my side, we negotiated a rent deal with Carl and his business partner, local dentist Joe Chau. (Carl skilfully used Joe in negotiations, with: "You know, Bob, you're a mate and if it was just up to me you know I'd agree to that lower price, but Joe is such a hard bastard.") Partners do come in handy sometimes.

The problem was that the video store owners, Dennis and Tina Lucas, had the existing lease, and, because video stores were falling over with the advent of online streaming, they wanted to quit their obligations as quickly as possible.

I liked the Lucas family. Real goers. They went from one store in the Huon Valley to a chain around the state (although Blockbuster was an American franchise). And later they were smart enough to recognise video days were limited and diversify into motor home rentals, Cruisin' Motor Homes, with offices all around Australia.

But there's no liking or love in business. I had to have a lease that stated the agreement was subject to gaining approvals from the local council (Clarence again) for a 24-hour, 7-days-a-week gym, and I knew there may be problems with the 24-hour part. I was also smart enough to put in the lease that I needed to gain not only all council planning approvals but also all statutory authority go-aheads (such as building and plumbing permits), which can often take lots of frustrating time after the main planning gets the green light.

The Lucases signed in June. It would be another nine months before we opened, and the initial goodwill disintegrated as they found themselves paying the rent on an empty store. In some ways I don't blame them, but I also didn't want to be forking out rent before I needed to. Unfortunately, as these things often do, the matter eventually ended up in court. The Lucases had already closed the store but left a tangle of shelving, glued carpet tiles, security gates and other paraphernalia.

Dennis had taken off to attend to another store he owned in Geelong in Victoria. He was hard to contact.

The council couldn't get its head around a 24-hour gym. What about accidents? No supervision, noise, youth crime, theft, rape, deaths, pestilence... you name it. One councillor was convinced young people would use it for late night parties; another was adamant it would be a front for bikie gangs dealing in drugs. When we met and they realised there were no change rooms or lockers – just two unisex showers – the sexual assault and robbery theories exploded.

"The police will need to patrol it all night," one said. "You'll need to pay for the cost of extra police."

"And where will people leave their valuables?" another demanded.

When I confessed that they would be out in the open in $99 storage cubes purchased from discount store Fantastic Furniture, there was pandemonium.

Yet another wanted to make it male only to protect females from rape and sexual assault. "There's already female-only gyms, so why not male-only?" she insisted.

Luckily, one of the perceived biggest hurdles – insurance cover for an unsupervised gym that never shut – was overcome when a local insurance broker, Mark West, managed to convince an underwriter to back us. This was mainly because we agreed to install sixteen surveillance cameras – and also provide a direct line to police and ambulance. (The "direct line" to police and ambulance actually went to a security company, who then had to phone the emergency services, meaning a sizeable time lapse before arrival.) Also, there was a mandatory defibrillator and we provided lanyards with emergency buttons for members to wear late at night if desired.

One of the amazing legacies of 24-hour gyms is that they generate fewer insurance claims than conventional gyms. The sixteen to twenty surveillance cameras act as a great deterrent; incredibly, there are fewer thefts than in separate change rooms with lockers because would-be thieves know their crime will be there for all to see on camera. We've never had a theft in a Zap gym – and that's more than I can say for Club Silly Wanker, where thefts are also higher because members think they're out of sight in change rooms. Rather than taking up police resources, we've actually helped them many times by supplying footage from our outside video cameras to help combat unrelated crime in the streets nearby. In fact, my insurance company later admitted that they'd rather insure Zap, with all its cameras, than so-called full-service, restricted-hours gyms that pretend to supervise members. Yeah right, except when staff go to lunch or the toilet or even to sleep.

When I was able to tell council that we had been cleared by an insurance company, their attitude softened slightly. But the real factor was that the GFC had hit Australia and every council wanted to avoid empty buildings and get the economy moving. Although there was still resistance, it was a bad look to knock back budding business entrepreneurs in this climate, even if they were sixty-five years old.

When the council finally, reluctantly, gave approval they had no idea of the fitness tsunami they had just unleashed. There were some restrictions, such as the maximum number of people in the gym at any one time (impossible to ascertain anyway), but nothing we couldn't handle. Nothing except the Lucas family; there, conditions worsened, tempers frayed. I stayed on my bike and kept pedalling. Dennis, ensconced in Geelong, heard about the council approval and immediately demanded rent from the approval date. "Sorry, Dennis, we haven't got the statutory permits yet." Thank God I put in those clauses.

Because we had council approval, I was keen, while waiting for the building and plumbing permits, to do some preliminary work to make sure we could hit the ground running when those permits were finally issued, and preferably to avoid opening around Christmas. Dennis refused. Sadly, he sued us for deliberately holding up the project to avoid paying rent. He was badly advised by his lawyers. We were able to prove – with copies of emails and letters – that far from trying to hold up the project, we'd pushed council officers to approve the application as fast as they could. The case was thrown out.

To his credit, Dennis came up and apologised afterwards and said he'd been misled by his legal team. He shook my hand and wished us well. I bore no grudges. The great thing was that the next decade would see both parties come out on top – me with Zap and the Lucas family with Cruisin' Motor Homes.

It was December 2008, and we were ready to go. The business landscape was barren, with gloom and doom all around; but, as I've said before, it's all about luck and timing.

The GFC had begun in mid-2007. And governments, desperate to get the economy moving again, were now providing great tax incentives. Luck and timing. We were due to open on 2 March 2009. The GFC ended almost exactly on that date.

And, Dad, I was pedalling flat out.

WORKOUT 12

GET THE FIRST ONE RIGHT

When you're embarking on a new business venture it's important to do the first one – even if it's the only one – right. There are no second chances. The public will judge you on first appearances and either support your business – or not.

Don't be a cheapskate and skimp on materials or quality, even if it takes every cent you've got. Otherwise, your brand will be diminished and you may never recover.

The Zap site battle may have been over – but things didn't get any easier. We ran an advertorial in the local suburban newspaper, the *Eastern Shore Sun*, which excitedly extolled the virtues of Tasmania's first 24-hour gym. Trouble was, down in Sandy Bay for many years there had been a rundown hole-in-the-wall gym with archaic equipment scattered over the dingy interior. Apparently, according to the owner, members (probably all fifty of them) had a key and they could get in after hours. So, he maintained, we weren't Tasmania's first 24-hour gym. And he threatened to sue if he didn't get an apology and a retraction in the paper. I felt like saying it's Tasmania's first 24-hour *gym* – not rat hole – but ignored him instead. The claim didn't really matter because to the population it was the first 24-hour gym they'd ever seen or heard of.

Our advertising was basic – no social media in those days, just catchment area mail drop and local papers. Plus, good old everybody-knows-everybody (maybe we are all related) word of mouth.

The Rosny gym was revolutionary, not only for Tasmania but also for Australia. Thankfully, we weren't tied to an American franchise model. We could let it all run free and be our creative selves. Here's why:

Charges: We decided to charge $8.95 a week – or $17.90 on a fortnightly direct debit from bank account or credit card. This was about half of what our competitors charged and one third of the $27.95 a week charged by the up-market Club Silly Wanker, with its pool, spa and steam room.

Joining fees: I always loathed joining fees in the fitness industry; they smacked of rip-off and people were very cynical about them. So we charged a "key fee" of $69.90 – which I know was a pseudo joining fee but at least it sounded better.

Four weeks upfront: Oh, yes, we also asked people to pay the first four weeks up front (four x $8.95 = $35.80) but then they got the last four weeks free after they cancelled. This was, I must admit, a clever ploy because when people cancel, they usually don't worry about the last four weeks. But it really helped our cash flow.

Cancel any time: Apart from 24/7, this was our great selling point. Cancel any time – unheard-of in the industry, trail-blazing. Ours was a genuine immediate cancel – unlike that of our eventual 24-hour competitors, who insisted on two to four weeks' notice.

Genuine numbers: Most gyms counted suspensions and redundant members in their numbers. Zap was pure and unadulterated. We counted only financial members who were paying each fortnight.

No fights: Most clubs to that point had insisted members join for twelve months or anything up to three years. And if anyone wanted to cancel, they had to pay a hefty penalty, which resulted in arguments, fights, court cases and even fisticuffs. I had learned my lesson all those years ago at Dockside.

No long terms: I actively discouraged people from paying for twelve months up front. I wanted my gym to operate on a fortnightly basis and if people didn't like us, they could quit straight away – no questions asked or disagreements. We lived or died by our reputation; no locking people in for years.

No suspensions: The other controversial decision I made was not to allow suspensions. From the early 1980s, fitness centres had made the mistake of allowing people to suspend their membership whenever they went on holiday or wanted time off. Except for genuine medical reasons, this was ridiculous. My reasoning was that if people went on holiday for two to four weeks, they'd keep paying their membership when it was only $8.95 a week. If the member did cancel, the critical factor was to make it expensive for them to rejoin. They would have to pay a new key fee of $69 – usually more costly than letting the membership run on. I could never understand the logic of Australia's biggest club chains almost encouraging cancellations by letting members rejoin for nil joining fee. Idiotic. That almost encourages people to quit, knowing it's easy to come back.

Transparency: The other thing I insisted on was complete transparency with pricing. We had nothing to hide; it was all good news. Until Zap revolutionised the fitness business, sales consultants would be sacked if they handed out the price over the phone; or, heaven forbid, emailed the details. The idea was to force the prospect to come into the gym so they were corralled and could be shown around the "state-of-the-art" facilities. People were treated like fools. "I just want the bloody price," frustrated prospects would scream. "Don't blame me, it's our policy," the huffy salesperson would reply. Sorry, they did blame you. Our prices were clearly displayed on our website, so people knew immediately what they were up for.

Consistency: The onus was on us to make every Zap the same high-quality operation so people would know what they were getting without having to tour the gym. This helped a short time later when we were the first gym in Australia to introduce the ability to join online. People knew Zap – the design, layout, equipment and what it stood for – so they had no hesitation joining sight unseen.

Of course, I knew even before the first Zap opened that another major advantage would be my motto: "Join one, join them all"; or, as it became later, when we reached twenty-three in Tasmania, "Join one Zap and get 22 gyms free." My old catch-cry of "one on every street corner" was very nearly true.

Our main dot points on the first double-sided A4 flyer were:

- Costs less than three cups of coffee a week
- Open 24 hours a day, 7 days a week
- Even work out on Christmas Day
- Your own private gym
- No long waiting lines (thankfully, for the bottom line, that turned out not to be the case)
- Same price for life (as long as you remain a member)
- World class equipment
- Cancel any time.

People couldn't believe it. But would it be a shit sandwich with sub-standard equipment? Well, no, we had the best equipment brand in the land – Life Fitness. There were definitely no frills: but the equipment was great.

Many gyms try to do fancy layouts with equipment spread out in clusters around the floor, making it frustrating and difficult for members to find what they're looking for. My theory was that people were there for a damn good workout and didn't want fancy add-ons. So, we went with a basic cardio layout of four lines of six to eight pieces of equipment: treadmills, cross-trainers, stationary upright bikes and recumbents; and a few spin bikes for good measure. The strength area was free weights with multiple pin-loaded machines – plus a small stretching area.

The reception desk was white and tiny. Two small red couches bought cheaply from Fantastic Furniture made up the members' area. No space to sit and relax; we wanted people to have a workout and go home. Hate to say it, but we didn't even provide a desk chair for our manager. We wanted them walking around the gym talking to people, not slumped in front of a computer doing private assignments.

And the best part for a business owner: we needed just one person working 10am to 2pm and 2.30 to 6.30pm Monday to Thursday; 10am to 2pm Friday and Saturday; and we were unstaffed on Sundays.

My loyal sales supremo, Meg, and I were playing around with layouts one night – virtually hand drawn on foolscap paper with biros – when Meg said, "Leave it with me, I'll get back to you tomorrow."

Did she ever. And it was a work of art, beautifully drawn in artists' colours with brush marks and squiggles and scrawls and flourishes. At first glance it looked like *Blue Poles*. But upon deeper examination it was a full-colour gym layout in all its glory... reds and whites and yellows. Meg summoned all her creative juices and the result – with a few changes – became the Zap layout for most of our gyms. The only mistake she made was selecting a very expensive red paint variety (I didn't realise there were more than 100 shades of red). It was an artists' paint – Durapern red – and it cost a fortune each time we opened a new gym. But it looked a treat.

During the fit-out phase, the interior of our first Zap looked like someone had just removed the lid from a box of ants, with workers scurrying in every direction: colliding occasionally, but mostly focused on the job at hand. Dr Strangelove and Ned Kelly were draped in wires and cables and holding court in the middle of the chaotic building site. This always worried the hell out of me. When I interjected, they'd talk the Freak Factory lingo and, not wanting to look completely stupid, I'd nod my head and slink away.

Contractors worked well into the night to meet the deadline of our

2 March opening. Mostly, it was appreciated – except for one incident. I came in about 10pm to check on progress. Seated in the middle of the gym was Ned, surrounded by a group of about fifteen people. It looked like some sort of seance, except they were mysteriously rubbing away at magic lanterns... and many beer bottles already littered the floor.

"What's going on, mate?" I asked.

"We're just cleaning the fluorescent light covers," replied Ned, in his usual affable style.

"Who's we?"

"Ah, mate, just got a few friends and relations to help me. Big job you know, Bob."

"Who told you to do that, Tim?"

"No one, mate, but you know it needed doing."

"Am I paying them, Tim?"

"Ah, mate, don't worry, I'll just put it on the account."

"How much are we paying them, Tim?"

"$35 an hour. After hours, you know, mate."

Rapid-Fire Robert did a rough calculation of $35 x 15 = $525 probably for at least four hours = $2,100. RFR wasn't pleased. In fact, he exploded.

"Bloody well get 'em out of here... I didn't ask you to do it... I'm not financing your relations' next overseas holiday," I erupted.

There were no more affable "mates" thrown in to the conversation. The friends and relations left, with great umbrage and mutterings about that prick Bob and how they hoped the gym failed.

No way was it going to fail, mate.

On opening day the first Zap looked a treat. Emblazoned with logos and red-and-white and slogans and the web address, the premises stood out like the Opera House. Just as I'd hoped. After much discussion about a slogan, we had decided on the rather mundane "Workout night and day", to reinforce the 24-hour message.

We didn't believe in opening ceremonies, getting the local mayor

There's no greater feeling in this world than the satisfaction of having a go at something and seeing it succeed.

to cut a ribbon, or even champagne and carrot cake. This was Zap. It stood on its merits. More important, we couldn't handle the crowds. By the time the door was officially zapped we had 700 members. I'd budgeted on 720 – two members per square metre – and this was only the first day. (We ended up with 1,800 members at five per square metre.) We had just unveiled what was to become the most successful per-square-metre gym in Australia, with the nation's best profit margin. In little old Tassie. Same as I'd done with the Eastern Shore Indoor Cricket centre twenty-six years before, I stood out in the crowded car park and let my pride glow brighter than the Zap signs illuminated above. There's no greater feeling in this world than the satisfaction of having a go at something and seeing it succeed.

We finally headed down to the local Chinese restaurant at Bellerive late at night – Meg and I, Strangelove, and Gazza – one of our personal trainers (Gaz was famous for always answering our phone with the most succinct message in gym history: "Zap. Gaz.") We were exhausted but elated. Except Ned, who was still smarting from my dismissal of his cleaning brigade and refused to attend.

Later, I couldn't stop driving past the gym to see the giant Zap logos casting their magic spell – to me anyway – over the Eastern Shore. To make sure the Zap sign could be seen on the highway through the shops and trees, I travelled backwards and forwards over the Tasman Bridge, retracing my route over and over, until I became worried the cops would think I was a stalker. And I used my key to zap into the gym in the early hours of the morning to see how many people were working out (just two or three, but it still seemed like hundreds to this tired but happy old bloke).

Maybe I'd get my sweat-stained superannuation after all... without burdening the taxpayer.

Oh, yes, nearly forgot. I got a friend's three kids to clean the light covers. $1 a cover, total bill $35. Sorry, Ned, but you've got to be an "expenses bastard" when starting off a new business. Just read on.

BE AN EXPENSES BASTARD

S orry, all you touchy-feely warm-and-fuzzies out there: if you want to succeed in business – especially early on – you've got to be an expenses bastard. A real bastard. Tough and unrelenting and prepared to be unpopular – and, yes, even despised.

For a start, personally go through every invoice line by line; don't put up with generalised charges, such as "Work performed from 13 March to 10 April, including crap, bullshit, offal, waffle and whatever else I can think of to rip off this dumb idiot."

Send it back and ask for itemisation. Dispute every detail if you're not happy. Negotiate another price if necessary. And, you know what? Suppliers and contractors and professionals respect you more for that. They know you're no pushover, and they know they'll have a fight on their hands if they don't get it spot-on.

Another apology to the many people from all walks of life and occupations that I've dealt with over the years: when you're starting off a business you must not pay within thirty days. It sounds callous, but you must push it out to sixty or ninety days, or as long as you can until the threat of legal action and phone calls gets too much. The only exceptions, of course, are the heavies: tax office, ASIC, state government and councils, and any other instrumentality you have no chance of resisting without heavy penalties.

It's usually the smaller accounts and operators who make the most noise: they need the money. So, when their nuisance effect – phone calls, visits, threats, disruptions – gets too much, pay them and rely on the bigger accounts to carry you through the early days.

Now that you're over the shock of what being an expenses bastard really means, remember this: the greatest business alliances – trust, loyalty and, yes, friendships – are built from early stoushes over costs. And if hostilities get too much, move on to someone else.

Here are some examples.

I didn't get on with most of the contractors I used for the first Zap gym, at Rosny. Some of it was being an expenses bastard, but relationships didn't gel and there were always tensions.

I sacked the builders halfway through because I thought they were overcharging on the bathrooms; in the end we managed to use pumps instead of digging up floors and saved many thousands.

The Freak Factory was an exception: There was very little trust, but, as outlined before, I was totally dependent on them and their contractors. With the others I could move on to other suppliers.

Signs were an example: The Rosny signs were installed by well-regarded Hobart business Eye Spy signs, who did a great job, and the owner was a good bloke. But he was very aggressive about the accounts and in the end the relationship fell apart.

I moved on to Claude Neon and Mike Elliott, a former Sandy Bay football champion, whom I knew from those days. We had our moments early on, but in the end, we became great friends and shared

The greatest business alliances are built from early stoushes over costs.

enormous goodwill. After the first few Zap installations I trusted Mike so much I didn't even bother getting a quote for each new job. He knew exactly what I wanted, and I knew he wouldn't try to rip me off. If the account went more than thirty days, he wasn't on the phone being hyper aggressive. Mike also handled outdoor signage and I decided early on that billboards would be a big part of Zap's advertising and brand building; they couldn't be turned off like a TV. Mike played a major role in getting us the best sites for our signs, at the best price. Why? Because we had forged trust and loyalty and it was a pleasure to do business.

My greatest business relationship was with Wayne Palmer and his company, Home and Commercial Maintenance. Wayne had worked his way up to start his own company after doing maintenance at the University of Tasmania and he'd been Club Silly Wanker's "pool maintenance man" after hours. I turned to Wayne when we did our second Zap at Moonah. We had a disagreement over the price he charged for the cardio floor (the raised area that housed all the electronic machines). Actually, it was more than a disagreement; it was war. I wanted the cardio area – an extremely important part of the Zap layout – built from chipboard with a floating floor over the top. Due to a misunderstanding Wayne did the "shell" in good timber as well and charged me what I considered "a fortune". I wasn't happy.

After I had refused to pay the bill, Wayne rang me late one night and said, "I think it's best if we cut our ties on Zap and don't do business any more."

"Are you sure that's what you want?" I certainly didn't.

He let fly again, and so did I. That's it then, I thought, as we both hung up on each other at the same time.

Next morning, Wayne rang back more conciliatory... and I realised I had gone too far. Thank goodness we called a truce and worked out a fair deal. Out of the wreck we forged one of the great business relationships. He's now one of my greatest mates and he's one of the few people in this world who is 100 per cent loyal and whom I trust absolutely. I'm friends with his family: wife Annette, sons Jack and Ryan, and daughter Ashlee. Wayne is also one of the first blokes I'd pick to be in the trenches beside me, if it ever came to that. My trust was so absolute that for most of the sites I'd select – including in Melbourne – I'd show him the building plans and say, "There you go, mate, go and do it." All I would ask for was an estimate. Wayne and his team would always bring it in on budget, do an outstanding job and, most importantly, take pride in their work to make sure it was exemplary. Without him I couldn't have made Zap the success it became.

So, be an expenses bastard. From the fire, you can forge great respect and lifelong business relationships. And, most importantly, you will ensure your business is a success – especially in the early days, when it's make or break.

HOW TO SNARE YOUR PREY

For most big gyms, selling fitness is a military-style operation full of devious traps and trickery more akin to a well-organised crime syndicate than caring about prospective members' welfare.

Dubious, high-powered American sales systems inevitably found their way into Aussie gyms in the late 1980s. In fact, most of the gyms were built on grabbing sales regardless of cost or principles – with the new member as collateral damage. Their intent was not to get people fit but to make money. They were labelled "agents of change" – as in changing people's lives – but the only change they were interested in was the change they could put in their pockets (and not small either).

They trained staff in body language, scripts and role-playing; and, more important, the close, which ended any hope the unfortunate

Consultants were taught not to close the door – in case the prospect panicked. But usually, the poor soul was trapped behind glass like a fish in an aquarium.

prospect had had of escaping unharmed. Greetings were well-rehearsed: smile, open palms, eye-contact, sincere tone and "welcome to the club". Personal trainers were synchronised to walk past with a wave as the prospect was lured into the lair – I mean, sales office. Consultants were taught not to close the door – in case the prospect panicked. But usually, the poor soul was trapped behind glass like a fish in an aquarium, with the Great White Sales Shark circling for the kill.

Following this model, you'd find consultants trotting out catch phrases, honed over many sales training courses, such as "Can you see yourself training here?" And during the tour, they'd be sure to put the prey – I mean, prospect – on a piece of equipment and say, "Feels good, doesn't it?" This is known in the industry as a tie-down. (The language is the same as that used to sell real estate.)

By now the victim is likely too scared, confused and intimidated to resist signing up for twelve months, with a fee for personal training on top. The consultants smile as they circle the most expensive option, always moving the pen left to right down the page, and never using dollar signs in front of the figures in case the poor soul suddenly realises they are parting with real money, not playing noughts and crosses.

And finally the death mantra: "Do you want to use Mastercard, Visa or Amex?" Sign here. The punters don't stand a chance.

Of course, the upfront twelve-month membership is mercilessly flogged (money in the bank), loaded with promises of personal training and extra support – all of which come at a cost. Once a member is signed up for twelve months or more, only death will get them out of the contract (and not even that in some cases).

And the joining fees? Gyms present themselves like exclusive golf clubs or country clubs where there's a genuine waiting list to become a member; not desperate, as in fact they are, to recruit as many as possible. Joining fees are good earners: a monetary figure always $1 short of the rounded hundreds – $99 or $199. Or, if you wait until the end of the month when consultants are desperate to make target, you can get it for zero. As mentioned, sales people are forbidden to give out membership prices over the phone: you have to make the appointment "belly to belly". Closing ratios have to be at 75 per cent for them to keep their job.

Another popular trick is to grant free workout time – but the membership form has to be filled in for their personal liability during this time. And, oh yes, we'll need all your banking details for security as it's a private club. As soon as the free time is up – wham! bam! your bank account is docked.

International students are a great source of revenue. First, they bring lots of uni friends; second, they keep paying after they return home to China or wherever (having forgotten to cancel); third, they always pay the full joining fee with their parents' credit card. Full commission for the gym commandos.

If all else fails, the consultant trots out: "I'll have to go to see my manager to see if I can give you a discount" – even though the apparent discount is the actual selling price in the first place and the manager has gone home.

The obligatory handwritten "thank you" cards are churned out at night (part of the sales checklist) – probably the last personal contact the member will ever have from the gym. Unless, of course, they fall for the "lose weight today" free personal training pitch. These free sessions are structured so that, by the last one, the client is totally dependent on the trainer for their exercise program, like a mother suckling a newborn baby. Some gyms even throw in a free ten-minute massage at the end to make sure the client is ensnared in the web. And let's not forget about the orchestrated wave-and-laugh across the gym floor from the consultant who put you there in the first place. All warm and fuzzy, eh?

It's all about selling on emotion and taking advantage of the walk-in's desperate need to get fit, lose weight and feel good about themselves. After signing on the dotted line, the new member walks out with nothing but hollow promises of a new body and life – not even a piece of paper.

It's all intangible – like an insurance policy. They get home and wonder what the hell they've done. Most people don't realise that you have to be disciplined to make a membership work – spend at least three times a week in the gym. It's hard yakka and there's no magic pill. Most people fall by the wayside after a short time. Some even try to get their money back. Fools. No chance. The membership consultants have their commission; who cares what happens next?

I'm embarrassed to say I embraced these practices at both Dockside and Club Silly Wanker because, well, everyone did it that way, and the bigger full-service gyms still do to this day. They have to fill the POPs. I was determined Zap would chart a different course; we were going to have transparency and integrity, even though selling was important. We were going to use Meg's skills to get people through the door and then they could make up their own minds without being pressured – or conned.

Zap was going to be different. Of that I was certain.

IT'S THE PROFIT, STUPID

During Bill Clinton's successful United States presidential campaign in 1992, his chief strategist, James Carville, coined the phrase "It's the economy, stupid". It was designed to embarrass the incumbent president George HW Bush, because Bush had failed to do anything about a recent recession. It quickly became a slogan.

Clinton had the slogan hung as a sign outside his campaign headquarters in Little Rock, Arkansas, and never strayed from the message. It worked a treat as he won easily.

I'd like to hang the same sign – substituting "profit" for "economy" – in the office of every gym owner in the country. Because if you're not making a profit you won't be in business very long.

I don't believe in the self-serving, verbose, meaningless mission statements that every business trots out to try to justify its existence. But if I did, mine would simply read: Make A Profit. Basic, eh? It's amazing how many businesspeople don't seem to worry about profit. Put simply, it means taking in more money than you pay out. Duh!

In the gym industry, owners get caught up in massive egos, over-servicing, coming up with all sorts of free trendy new programs and giveaways to make members love them – completely forgetting that the cost doesn't justify the means. They become seduced by the glamour and excitement – geez I might even get on the front page of our industry magazine – and forget that it's all about hard work, and profit margins.

Sure, if you must, have some member functions outside the gym (just know that only about 5 per cent of your membership will attend, and they're usually the ones who are rusted on), but don't become obsessed with in-house hospitality or breakfasts and functions all in the name of retaining members.

What retains members are the three WELLs: a *well*-located, clean gym; *well*-serviced equipment that is never out of action for more than a day; and *well*-coming, friendly staff. Forget about the rest.

When I talk to gym owners I simply ask: How much profit are you making? Silence. Half don't even know; or they mumble something about having a $2 million business. Two-million-dollar business? I become exasperated when the media writes about some alleged business success story and gush that it's a $10 million business. People immediately think, wow, they're making $10 million profit – or the business is worth $10 million. But no. They mean they have a $10 million turnover; they don't know the difference between profit and revenue. It's easy to turn over $10 million; keeping it is what counts. These establishments could be just breaking even, or losing money.

And, while I'm on it – bin the business plans. When someone is thinking about opening a new business, they rush to do *the* business plan. What a waste of time. You have to know what you intend to do, and how it's going to be achieved. But don't spend weeks on

Rent is the major cost: once it gets over 20 per cent of revenue you know you have problems.

computer-templated, waffling, padded, never-achieve business plans – unless your bank insists.

I was forced to hire accountants to draw up a business financial plan for Zap – only because my bank insisted on it before agreeing to provide hire purchase finance for our equipment. It was targeted to finance but wasn't worth the paper it was written on. All bullshit, figures plucked out of the air. You can make up anything you like to satisfy some desk-bound bank Johnny or Josephine – but putting it all into action is what counts. My "secret" business plan for Zap consisted of one sheet of A4 paper with dot points outlining what I wanted to achieve: clear, concise, to the point.

The same goes for annual budgets. You can fantasise all you want – and let wishful thinking rule your mind – but if you don't achieve the ambitious figures you've spent weeks laboriously putting on paper, you'll feel depressed. And so will your financiers if they get to see it. In my entire time with Zap I never did a budget. My aim was to run the business as lean and mean as possible, and to bring in maximum revenue through smart advertising and marketing. Why do you need a budget? From day one, I told all staff that I wanted Zap to be a media company selling fitness. Use smart digital marketing to bring in the revenue and provide good facilities, and the rest will take care of itself.

The other dollar drain that gym owners get carried away with is paying big commissions to rapacious sales staff, as discussed in

Workout 14. A lot of bad practices are caused by paying consultants commissions on new-member sales targets – but not taking into account the cancellations. In Zap gyms we didn't really need to incentivise staff because memberships sold themselves; but in our bigger gyms it was always based on net gain each month – not new members. That way our staff were intent on saving memberships and preventing cancellations just as much as getting new members.

To make it foolproof I also had a lag time of two months on commissions – so if you underperformed the following month after making a net gain, you got nothing until you exceeded the original target. That also stopped staff from bringing forward membership sales to make target on the last day of the month – and then selling nothing for the first week of the next.

Another reason you don't need budgets in the fitness industry is that, once you get membership to the level you want, the cashflow is predictable. This is one of the glorious certainties in the gym game that you don't get in, say, retailing, where it's seasonal and you don't know what your takings will be from one day to the next. But you do need to micro-manage the expense ratios, especially when you begin operations. Know what profit margin you want, and make sure you achieve it.

Although I've never had business plans or budgets, I'm a great jotter and scribbler. I'm always fiddling around with figures, either in my Day-Timer diary (yes I have used hard copy Day-Timers for the past twenty-five years). And I've always done basic five-year personal plans – about eight to ten dot points – updated every year. With Zap it was an evolving feast as I worked on figures and ratios every day, calculating what my profit margin should be.

I decided I wanted a 35 per cent bottom line – unheard of in the industry, where it's usually 10 per cent at best or, more frequently, in the red. So, I doodled and dashed away in the Day-Timer most days. The fitness industry is easy in this regard. It carries very little stock (and what it does carry – T-shirts, drink bottles and accessories – usually loses money through theft and lack of turnover); has a predictable cashflow with direct debits coming in every week or fortnight; and outgoings can be large but straightforward. The certain cashflow, low staffing levels, and relatively few expenses are what make gyms such great businesses – and easy to run – once you get the members through the door. And if you know what you're doing.

I worked on 8 per cent of the population within a 5-kilometre radius joining our gym. I also figured our gyms would take two members per square metre. That would be rather crowded if they all came at once; but don't forget members stop and start – and they come in over a 24-hour period, seven days a week. (Monday is always the busiest day. Usually 22 per cent of total membership attend on Monday, to work off the weekend's indulgences.) So, if you have, say, a population of 10,000 within 5 kilometres of your gym, then 8 per cent would be 800 members. I know this is simplistic, but that's what ratios need to be. And they worked for Zap.

In Melbourne, with a higher population density, we found we needed to make the radius 3 kilometres to be conservative. And for every opposition 24-hour gym in the catchment area that was half-decent (most are crap), we'd deduct a percentage point off the 8 per cent.

The basic recurring diary ratios looked like this: rent 20 per cent; wages 10 per cent; leasing 15 per cent; other, such as insurance, bank fees (high because of direct debits) 20 per cent; profit margin 35 per cent. Simple. And I made it work. But you've got to be messianic about it.

Rent is the major cost: once it's over 20 per cent of revenue you know you have problems. I used to aim for no more than 10 per cent and we got that at Rosny and repeated it at our second and fourth Zap gyms, Moonah and Kingston. If you've worked out decent ratios you know immediately whether your rent is too expensive when negotiations take place.

Working on 800 members, and a membership price of, say, $600 a year (based on a $12-per-week membership) you know your total membership revenue will be $480,000 a year; add on key fees and

Gyms are the "pubs" of the twenty-first century.

other additional items, such as personal trainers rental, and you'll get $600,000. Therefore, if you're paying more than $120,000 (20 per cent of $600,000) a year for rent, including outgoings, it won't work; and of course, you aim for $90,000 (15 per cent). With these simple calculations in his head, Rapid-Fire Robert usually reigned supreme in negotiations.

The only exception to this rule is if you want a signature gym in an affluent or high-density suburb to promote your brand. To do this, you must be willing to pay more rent, forgo some profit, and see the extra as billboard advertising. The other reason to do it is to keep out opposition in a critical area that you want to dominate (more of that later in Workout 17). For instance, when we decided to expand to Melbourne – where at that stage no one knew the brand, and billboard advertising was prohibitive – we paid exorbitant rents in a few blue-ribbon suburbs on busy thoroughfares, such as Glenferrie Road in Hawthorn, to establish our presence. (Thank goodness for our unapologetic bold and brassy business signage and branding.)

Rosny turned out to be a perfect place to have opened our first Zap. With a population of about 55,000 on Hobart's Eastern Shore – and very little competition – it was a licence to print money. As mentioned, we jammed more than 1,800 members into an area of 360 square metres and that made Rosny the most profitable gym in Australia.

Another great feature of the gym industry is that atmosphere is important – especially for the under 40s. For them, there's nothing worse than an empty gym; they love the vibe of crowded areas, chatting up girls and boys and making new friends. Who cares about a workout when you've got the mobile number of someone you fancy? When I was young, we used to go to the pub to socialise. Gyms are the "pubs" of the twenty-first century.

But don't get carried away: always remember you're in business to make a profit, not to go through the motions. Work out your ratios and margins before you start, and be relentless in trying to achieve them.

MAKE THE MOST OF COMFORTABLE ANXIETY

always wake up early – 3.40am to be exact. Right on the dot. It doesn't matter if I go to bed at midnight or even later, summer or winter, I still wake up at the same time.

Usually, I like to hit the sack no later than 10pm, read about three pages of my current book (takes a long time to finish books at that rate, but there are plane trips to speed things up) and then lights out. By that time I'm so tired I can hardly flick the switch. I exist on four to six hours' sleep a night; at weekends I may take a nap in the afternoon while watching the footy or cricket on TV; but even on Saturdays and Sundays I wake at that magic hour of 3.40.

After I open my eyes, I spend twenty minutes in what I've termed my State of Comfortable Anxiety (SOCA for short). This is my time of suspended business animation. As soon as I gain consciousness I worry about what has to be done for the day: the problems I face, the hard phone calls I have to make, the threats to the business, staff problems – anything challenging that floats into my head. At first there's panic: shit what a bastard of a day this is going to be. That phone call, that meeting, what the hell am I going to do? I lie there as the stress starts to mount. Will the business survive these twenty minutes of negative thought? Yet, confronting as it can be, I'd still never give up my SOCA time.

During those 1,200 seconds of worry time, I manage to put it all in perspective. Hey, I'm alive, I'm fit and healthy. Dad, I'm still pedalling. Sandy, I'm going to say "Good morning God." I'm still worried and anxious about the day ahead, but I can handle it, I'm comfortable with it. In other words I've become comfortable with being uncomfortable. Yes, I've reached my SOCA.

And, as I throw off the sheets at 4am, the comfortable anxiety becomes even more comfortable. When you're on your feet and can do something about the worries of the day, it's amazing how they seem to melt away like a strawberry snow cone in the sunshine. There's nothing more beautiful than the morning sunrise. It's my time of day; full of promise and excitement, creativity and reflection.

Mind you, rising at 4am has had its problems over the years. Stephanie, as luck would have it, has never been a morning person and I've lived in fear of an alarm clock being thrown at me. One morning Stephanie's bedside clock crashed into the wall beside my head, glass and springs shattering. I was only a few millimetres away from certain death as I crept out in the darkness.

I was proud of the trendy violet, purple, blue and lime-green para-silk tracksuit uniform we used to wear when I first opened Dockside Fitness in the 1980s. But Steph, God bless her, claimed the pants rustled – *swish, swish, swish* – as I walked down our hallway shortly

If you want to start a business, you'll have to stop socialising and networking, because you won't have the time.

after 4am. And the tirade from a normally perfect lady was, well, unbecoming.

Then there was my daughter Melanie's vitriolic attack when, on holiday at our beachside shack at Cremorne, about 25 minutes south of Hobart, I still rose at my normal hour (alas, about five hours ahead of the rest of the family). Our pet Corgi, Zoe, followed suit and we trotted out to the kitchen together. Admittedly, the shack's wooden floorboards were a bit creaky, but Melanie's daily re-enactment of the scene that she honed to perfection over the years – *clump, clump, clump* (me) and *pitter-patter, pitter-patter* (Zoe) – always met with the usual sighs of exasperation over breakfast. And there were far-from-idle threats of everyone going back home without me if I didn't show more respect for family sleep-ins at the beach.

Am I tired after only a few hours' sleep every night? What's tiredness? All in the mind, I reckon. My first morning task is to make a cup of Dilmah extra-strength tea (I drink that and four cups of coffee by lunchtime). I focus on thinking, planning and emails until about 5.30am. Then I get in an hour's exercise until 6.30am (alternating weights in the home gym, bike riding, jogging or walking, depending on the state of my knees). I have breakfast and relax until 7.30am and then I start work proper.

I know who I can call at 7.30 (thank heavens for my fellow early risers), and those who don't start until (heaven forbid) 9am.

I try to finish work by 5pm and then unwind, usually with a glass of wine. And these days I eat out about five nights a week. After years of newspapers (where I worked until midnight), years of nightly parliamentary sittings and of the cocktail circuit, I'm afraid I've become rather boring.

Boring is right. If you want to start a business, you'll have to stop socialising and networking, because you won't have the time.

Business owners become obsessed with networking. You know, the old "you can't get ahead if you don't know the right people" and "climb the corporate ladder with contacts". I'm a shocking networker. I've mostly worked for myself, and if I had to rely on corporate "brown-nosing" and drinking with the right people to get ahead, I'd still be a copy boy at *The Mercury*.

As a politician I was forced to go to functions and cocktail parties. Usually I'd stand in a corner and find someone I knew to talk to. If I was forced to circulate, it usually ended in disaster. I'd introduce myself, as if for the first time, to people I'd met previously, much to their disdain. Or they'd say, "Hi Bob. You don't remember me, do you?" Stupidly I'd say, "Of course I do," while desperately searching my memory for their name as the conversation continued. They'd follow with: "Who am I, then?" After a few "I know your face" mumblings, I usually had to admit defeat. There goes another vote at the next election, I'd think.

I'm taller than most and going deaf, so in a noisy room I can't hear what the hell they're saying anyway.

My other pet hate is people trotting out the well-worn line "I work smarter, not harder." Do you now? Sorry, mate, that means you're lazy, and looking for excuses. I would never employ anyone with that attitude. What they should say is, "I have to work harder... and smarter." Without the "harder" you're never going to make it.

But, hey, all is good. Don't panic and stress about the day ahead: just reduce it to a State of Comfortable Anxiety and you can't go wrong. SOCA your way to success.

BUILD A FORTRESS TO REPEL INVADERS

Tassie is an island state – separated from mainland Australia by Bass Strait, one of the most treacherous bodies of water in the world.

As a wartime toddler – born in 1944 – I was always intrigued by small nails, or tacks, every few inches around the windows in our house at Evandale. Dad explained: "During the war everyone thought the Japanese would invade Tasmania and use it as a base to attack the rest of Australia. And so people nailed sheets of cardboard or masonite or whatever they could get hold of to cover up the windows so the Jap fighter planes couldn't see the lights at night."

Even as a trusting single-digit kid, I found the story implausible. But Dad insisted it was true.

"Why don't you take the tacks out now?" I asked.

"Ah, I reckon the wood's damaged and it'll look worse if I jemmy them out," was always the reply. "Besides, it's a reminder of how we could've been a Jap fortress," he added. "You're very lucky." So, they stayed as a symbol of our freedom.

After the successful opening of Rosny, my plan was, similarly, to turn Tasmania into a fortress – just Zap – not "Jap" (a disparaging term that was no longer used). Tassie was mine; I decided early on to do whatever it took to keep out the opposition. This was modern-day gym warfare, and I knew the US 24-hour franchises such as Anytime Fitness and another Aussie start-up, Jetts, would eventually begin invading Tasmania.

Thankfully (luck and timing again), Tassie back in 2009 wasn't the economic powerhouse it later became; it was viewed as a business wasteland to be avoided at all costs and considered only after mainland state opportunities had been exhausted. The most recent GFC only exacerbated the perception. But despite the parlous state of the economy, I knew some locals would look at getting one of the mainland franchises, especially once they became established. I had no time to waste.

The ambitious plan was to have fifteen Zaps open by June 2010; after Rosny this meant another fourteen in little more than a year. As it turned out, the fourteen became just four as I confronted the full force of Tassie's notorious council planning restrictions and red tape. When I was a politician I had tried, unsuccessfully, to reduce the number of councils and the unnecessary bureaucratic brick walls that held up development. Maybe some councillors were now taking revenge. Yes, I know, franchising may have been quicker and easier, because you had troops of would-be franchisees finding sites and helping out, but we were building a brand to be proud of and owning all our businesses.

Struggling video stores were still my main target, and Hobart's populous, blue collar northern suburbs of Moonah and Glenorchy were already in my sights.

The late Terry Ewing owned a chain of video stores around the state called Video City. Terry was fractious, volatile and unpredictable, but nonetheless had a large, prize site in Moonah that I decided I wanted (it would overtake Rosny as our most profitable gym, with 2,500 members). A smart businessman, Terry owned a lot of his premises and was able to profit from the downturn, and soften the closure of the video business, by renting out his strategic, well-located properties. I thought of owning our properties as well, but the plan for a rapid rollout of gyms meant I didn't have the time or money to put into a real estate portfolio.

Tassie – with twenty-seven local councils for a population of 500,000 (not to mention federal and state governments) – is the most over-governed and over-regulated jurisdiction in the western world. This means that you could sign leases on properties on the same day, but one might open six months ahead of the other; or, conversely, you might do the deals months apart but have the places open within a few days of each other.

That's exactly what happened with Moonah, and Devonport on the north-west coast, nearly 400 kilometres apart. They both opened in October 2009 and we had to travel between the two sites – nearly four hours by car. It's not much fun driving up the Midland Highway at midnight, tired and exhausted, with no food or sustenance, trying to open new gyms simultaneously.

In part, it was our fault. We used to launch our gyms on Mondays, and sales manager Meg (who later became CEO) and I were so possessive about our new arrivals that we would spend the weekend personally inspecting every centimetre of the gym to make sure it was perfect. We supervised the installation of equipment like arranging furniture in a new home. Nothing was left to chance.

I used to go to the local hardware store the day before we opened and personally buy rubbish bins, brooms, mops and anything else we

needed. It was only late on the Sunday night that I became satisfied our latest Zap was ready to be unveiled. Even the morning before each new gym opened, I would walk around the building, picking up any rubbish, checking on parking, feeling the excitement and anticipation of a new Zap entering the world.

It wasn't long before Tassie's gym jungle drums were beating to the news that Anytime Fitness had found a franchisee in Tasmania. Shit, I thought, it's happened sooner than I had hoped. Fortress Tassie was under attack, but boarding up our windows to keep out the lights wasn't going to work in the twenty-first century. The moat and walls had been breached; my SOCA moments were being tested.

Luckily, my fears were unfounded. Instead of opening in the more densely populated areas of Hobart, which were ripe for 24-hour gyms, the first Anytime Fitness opened in Launceston, a quaint, conservative bastion of 80,000 people about three hours away from the capital, where they still name modern single houses in the suburbs with monikers such as "Meadowbank" and "Stoney Rise", as if they were farms. Lonnie – as it's fondly known – had more gyms per head of population than any other city in Australia. It was a weird decision. And the franchisee lived in Hobart. Work that out. Predictably, the Launceston Anytime struggled, which bought us valuable time for the Zap rollout.

The fortress was challenged again some months later when I ran into a colleague in Hobart who said, "You're in trouble, Cheeky, there's a 24-hour gym opening in Battery Point near Club Salamanca. People are copying you." More attacks.

I found the proposed site, in Montpelier Retreat, only a block away from Club Silly Wanker, and used some long-held contacts to track down the owner, Adam Fisher, son of legendary Hobart property developer and alderman Barry Fisher. This is Tassie, remember: I knew him. The scenario improved further when Meg discovered she was a distant relation of his. We arranged a meeting in Adam's Battery Point office.

"Look, I'd like you to have the site, but I've got a signed lease with the Jetts franchisee," Adam explained. "You're too late, mate."

Shit. "Can't you do anything, Adam? Jetts is based in Queensland (even though the franchisee was a local pharmacist) and we want to keep this Tasmanian."

That hit home. "I'll see if I can get out of the contract," he said.

Later that day, Adam phoned to say he'd found a technicality and could break the contract. It was ours if we wanted it – on his terms, of course. Did I feel guilty about abusing the principles of contracts and fair play? No. This was business. The fortress had to be protected at all costs.

I paid a price, though. Adam's terms were horrendous – one of the worst lease deals I ever signed. Inflated rent to begin with and reviews every two years, pay all outgoings, no help with leasehold improvements, ratchet clause (to say the rent could never drop below its present value) … On it went. Nevertheless, I signed without hesitation. It was worth anything to keep out the opposition. And despite the high rent, the gym eventually became profitable – although it further drained Club Silly Wanker's bank balance as members left for the convenience of 24 hours and cheaper rates. But at least I was taking those members from myself.

It was a few years before the next Anytime attack. I'd just opened a smaller Zap in yet another of Terry Ewing's video stores, in North Glenorchy. It was a good site (ironically next door to a Hungry Jack's fast food outlet) but outside the main Glenorchy city area. I was always worried that left the door open for a competitor to move in by locating centrally.

And move in they did. Or tried to. This time the gym jungle drums reverberated from Melbourne, where a gym equipment colleague gave me the heads-up that Anytime had secured premises in the centre of Glenorchy. My fears had been realised.

More investigations. The building owner was none other than my friend Emmanuel Kalis, a genial but ruthless Greek businessman who had risen from humble potato merchant to leading Hobart property developer and hotel owner. EK, as he was known, had already custom built a Zap gym at Kingston for us, and we had a good relationship.

I got on the phone. "Emmanuel, mate, what are you doing to me? I hear you've sold me out and are letting the enemy into one of your buildings. You promised me you wouldn't rent your buildings to anyone other than Zap, mate."

"Ah, Bobby, mate," EK said in his distinctive thick Greek accent. "I offer that building to you, but you say you have better site down the road. I have to eat, Bobby."

Personally worth hundreds of millions, and portly from many sumptuous meals in his pubs, EK had no worries about where the next meal was coming from. But I got his point.

There was a reason I'd rejected his site. It was an office building (not preferred) and the site for lease sat immediately below another old-style, full-service gym – Health and Fitness World – which had been around a long time and had a loyal local following. I had no doubts we could run them out of business, but they served a different market and their premises were three times the size of EK's site. I didn't want to fight the locals by opening underneath. But I did need to keep the foreign insurgents out.

"Can you do *any*thing, mate?" I said to EK. "Have they signed yet?"

They had the contract but hadn't sent it back. Anytime Fitness was so desperate to get into Tasmania that it was prepared to open without a franchisee, under its company name. EK came good and helped keep out the enemy.

I didn't develop a Zap on the site for several years, during which time I did have to pay rent and outgoings for an empty building. But it was worth it to protect our territory. This made strategic sense. Rapid-Fire Robert worked out that if Anytime had opened I would have lost about 300 members from my existing nearby Zap – equalling roughly $200,000 a year. The rent on EK's empty building was about $120,000. So, I was better off to the tune of $80,000. And we halted the invasion yet again.

In time, we ended up taking over Health and Fitness World's area

Strategic acquisitions to thwart the enemy make perfect sense – even if you lose money... or at best break even.

as well as ours below, and opening our first Zap Mega – over more than 1,500 square metres and two floors. We still kept the one down the road.

Strategic acquisitions to thwart the enemy make perfect sense – even if you lose money on the manoeuvre or at best break even. Many people can't see that.

I did it again on the Eastern Shore. Earlier, we had taken over another small video store owned by Terry Ewing. It was in Clarence Street, Bellerive, next door to a bakery in a small two-shop location down the road from a bustling shopping centre, the Shoreline. I sensed danger if a Shoreline site became available. Sure enough, it did; and I pounced. It was high rent and only 400 metres from our other Zap – but better to be our own opposition. That was the only time I went into a shopping centre.

I looked on strategically placed multiple Zap sites in the one area as being like university campuses: even though they were separate, they were all part of Zap Shoreline. We changed the interiors slightly to make the smaller gym more focused on circuit training without machines. And in doing so we kept Fortress Tasmania buttressed. Without covering any windows – just our backsides.

Wherever you decide to invest, make it your own. Do whatever it takes to keep out the opposition.

WORKOUT 18

TRUST ONLY
YOURSELF

Some say business is built on trust. I say it's built on distrust.

In business, be wary of everyone. Most businesspeople will let you down in the end, especially if money's involved. And when they do, you don't want to be the sucker who has lost out because of blind faith. Sure, it would be nice to go to bed at night trusting everyone. Friends of mine say, "I'll trust them until they let me down." I turn this around: "Assume everyone is shonky until they prove otherwise."

People form a narrative in their own heads that justifies their actions, and there's no use pointing out how you've helped them, nurtured them, funded them, bled for them. Don't waste your breath.

There's an old saying in business: When you're CEO be nice to the junior office assistant because you may meet them again on your way down. In my experience, the former junior office assistant who has

Be wary of everyone. Most businesspeople will let you down in the end, especially if money's involved.

risen through the ranks will be the very one who knifes you – and, of course, conveniently forgets all the help you gave them when you were on top.

All very cynical, I know.

Apart from family, there are only four people in business I'd trust with my life: Wayne Palmer, boss of Home and Commercial Maintenance, who built our gyms; Joe Marguccio, former Life Fitness equipment area manager; Mike Elliott, of Claude Neon signs and billboards; and Zap shareholder and retired barrister and solicitor Steve Chopping, who always gave me unqualified support.

I remember coming out of politics without money (or super) and with Club Silly Wanker deep in the red. In desperation, I said to Steve: "I need to be paid a salary. I know we can't afford it right now, but I promise I'll make us profitable and will reward you in the end." He didn't hesitate. And when Zap was sold he got his reward – many times over.

I've spoken about how most business partners let you down. With employees it's usually that you hire them, train them, reward them... and then they go to the opposition down the road for a few more dollars or some other petty reason. Then there's other businesses who blatantly try to steal your ideas.

One of my Tasmanian landlords (let's call him Petrol Head), who I had come to know well, rang and said a friend of his from Queensland was interested in a Zap franchise. I pointed out we weren't franchising.

"Well he's interested in a partnership to develop Zaps in South Australia and Queensland. They want to fly down and talk to you."

I wasn't keen on the idea, but Petrol Head said the guy was a "great mate", and he would vouch for his integrity.

Three businessmen duly arrived in town, including Great Mate. Meg and I spent most of the day with them, including buying lunch, without giving much away of my hard-earned Zap formulas and systems. Then came dinner and the fact that they were staying the night. They were keen and they were likeable; there were two bottles of very good red on the table; and, after all, they had my landlord's guarantee of authenticity.

They again pressed about franchising. I wasn't ready and still resisted the notion, but there's no doubt the prospect of Zap going national was in the back of my mind.

With franchising off the agenda, they tried another tack: "Would you be interested in opening some Zaps in South Australia and we'll give you 20 per cent free carry (equity in the consortium) for the use of the brand and intellectual property?"

Not sure if it was Petrol Head's affirmations about Great Mate, or the wine, but my suspicions subsided, and I heard myself saying: "Make it 25 per cent and guarantee to build at least ten Zaps and we've got a deal."

Meg was the witness. We shook hands. Fatal mistake. Once upon a time, that meant something, but in modern business it can be sign language for "now see how much I can double-cross this naive idiot". Egged on by Great Mate and his cohorts, I stupidly proceeded to open up about Zap – including fishing out my laptop to proudly show how our systems operated.

The next morning I gave the three businessmen a lift to the airport, all buddies. More handshakes, and backslapping, as they boarded the plane with the promise that documentation consummating the deal would be forthcoming the following week.

Silence. Don't worry, Great Mate can be trusted – Petrol Head said so. Several emails later I finally received a reply. The three amigos had decided the "free carry" wouldn't work and they had decided to do it themselves, which they eventually did. Although not very well.

I rang Petrol Head and told him what I thought about his guarantees of Great Mate's integrity.

"Well, I haven't seen him for a while, but I guess that's business, Bob," he said.

Business indeed.

Not long after, another acquaintance who owned full-service gyms in Melbourne rang and said she and her husband were coming to Tasmania, were interested in opening 24-hour gyms in Victoria, and would like to look at our Zaps.

"Just let the staff know we'll be dropping in," she added.

Now, back in the 1980s and 90s it had long been a tradition for Aussie fitness centre owners to share ideas and visit each other's gyms when in town. There weren't that many of us and admittedly most of our clubs were exactly the same. But I'd spent a hell of a lot of time and effort developing the Zap brand, systems and formulas, and I wasn't about to let others come in and benefit for free.

When I said "No", there was silence on the other end of the phone before the line went dead. I later sat opposite her at a fitness convention dinner in the United States and the silence was again deafening. She and her husband eventually opened their own 24-hour gyms in Melbourne. Not as good as Zaps, but at least they did it themselves.

Never trust anyone until they earn that trust. And you'll find very few will.

WORKOUT 19

FEAR THE FAILED GYM OWNERS

don't like consultants – even though, after I sold Zap, I became one. My stint was more of a golden handcuff – to make sure I didn't get any ideas about starting another gym business to compete with my purchasers. Fat chance.

In the fitness industry, so-called consultants, sales trainers, marketing "experts", retention specialists (and the like) are usually failed gym owners who find it easier to tell other people how to run their businesses. Hopefully, they tell them to do the opposite of what they did. The big advantage is that they don't have to worry about putting their words of wisdom into practice.

Still, they're usually very good spruikers who can talk up their wares at conventions and trade shows with alarming sincerity. The worrying aspect is that all the young, starry-eyed newbie gym owners, and even desperate long-time stalwarts, hang on every word of every painstakingly choreographed, self-serving PowerPoint presentation.

The failed owners love being the centre of attention and not in a bankruptcy court, and they may well make some money this time around. But not at my expense, and hopefully not yours.

One such person, I'll call him Eddie, started an Australian version of one of business's most loved pastimes: roundtables, this time for the fitness industry. Roundtables are usually money-making exercises where "victims" in a certain industry or profession are invited to cough up some dough for the pleasure of sitting around a table for a couple of days to share ideas – but usually it's waffle about nothing and a "kick-on" every night at their favourite bar.

Just before I discovered Zap, when I was still running Club Silly Wanker, I was surprised to get a call from Eddie, whom I knew vaguely, inviting me to join his roundtable for gym owners (he must have been desperate). Some of the names were familiar, and it was held in Adelaide, so I thought at least I'll escape the morning member rumbles at Club Silly Wanker.

The star attraction was a Californian roundtable "expert", who looked like a portly Johnny Cash dressed all in black, which didn't do much for the mood of the meetings. Apparently he ran roundtables for lots of different occupations in the States, and he likely swotted up on what was happening in the fitness industry just before he left for Australia, and flew economy class to save us money, or so he said. Johnny and I didn't hit it off.

On arrival at the Adelaide venue we were all asked to fill in a card with personal questions about how we were feeling – with assurances that Johnny Cash and the Rounders were there to help with any problems. You had to rate your wellbeing out of 10.

Apart from the pressure of Club Silly Wanker, I was having some personal problems, and so scribbled down my true feelings like some adolescent teenager, rating myself 2 out of 10 on the wellbeing scale.

I looked forward to the promised support from my peers. Instead, I was immediately ushered into a room with Johnny and some other Rounders, where it was strongly suggested I should go home immediately because my depressed mood would ruin the next two days for other members. I assume they meant the nightly booze-up. I thanked them for their "support".

I stayed on. But wished I hadn't. Members were handing out their latest marketing campaigns – which I had run twenty years before at Dockside – while Johnny pontificated about some obscure Wyoming health club.

Suddenly, all hell broke loose. Eddie was on the roundtable as a gym owner (he hadn't closed his gym yet), and it was suddenly alleged that he was profiting out of the meetings (not sure how) without telling the other attendees. Argument raged for several hours – until a compromise was reached – then it was time for dinner, followed by a visit to a local strip club.

The next roundtable was held in Melbourne – and I apologised because I genuinely couldn't attend. But secretly I was thankful because I hadn't enjoyed the first. Johnny rang the next day, asked me to sit down and said he had some bad news. I braced myself, thinking someone had died.

"Sorry, Bob, but you've been sacked from the roundtable because of your lack of attendance, and because you don't contribute enough," Johnny solemnly said.

Another successful gym owner, Trish, was also sacked for the same reason. We rang each other afterwards and became good friends; and often laughed about Johnny and the Rounders. Thanks, Johnny. You did me a real favour by making me realise how deficient most other gym owners are and reinforcing my determination to forge a different path.

An old newspaper friend of mine used to say – in my view unkindly and unjustly – that Rotary clubs were places for self-made men and women to go and worship their makers. I'd say roundtables are unnecessary, indulgent talk fests where mediocre people go to tell each other how good they are.

I find most business organisations are a waste of time: just get on and run your own business without worrying about everyone else. But there are exceptions. IHRSA is the only fitness organisation worth joining. That said, the local version of IHRSA, Fitness Australia, does do some good work but is far too incestuous for my liking.

I've been a regular attendee at IHRSA conventions since 1994, when I went to Reno, in Nevada. Since then, I've attended about fifteen – in Los Angeles, Las Vegas, San Diego, Phoenix and San Francisco. They are always in the sunshine states so those in colder climates can escape the snow. The IHRSA trade show – as big as the MCG – is one of the highlights. I was usually a guest of my equipment supplier, Life Fitness.

In the early days, we were forced to share rooms. You'd be lying in bed late at night when some shadowy figure entered the room, rattled the coat hangers, dumped the bag and slipped under the covers. Next morning you'd find out who your roommate for the next few days would be. It was a time of great trepidation.

"How are you, mate? I'm Bill from Bill's Gym in Sydney."

One year, when the convention was in Phoenix, Arizona, I knew – for once – who I'd be rooming with: my mate from Life Fitness, Joe Marguccio, who looked after all our equipment purchases. Good news. At least we wouldn't fight.

I arrived first to discover our hotel room contained only one bed – a double. As you'd expect, the hotel was heavily booked for the convention. Staff said they'd attempt to get another twin room later but I should keep this one for now. Knackered after the fifteen-hour flight from Melbourne, I showered and fell asleep in the standard hotel bathrobe.

I awoke to the door opening and a loud yell, followed by the anxious footsteps of security guards, guns at the ready.

"Jesus Christ, I'm out of here," the voice shouted. It was Joe's.

Only take notice of people who can demonstrate they've been successful and profitable in their chosen fields.

The sight of this lanky gym owner reclining on the double bed in a bathrobe that had – unbeknown to me – fallen open at the front was too much for Joe. He spent the next hour demanding another room, in between explaining to the guards that I was actually his mate, and not a chainsaw murderer. The new room never arrived. For the next five nights, rather than share a double bed, Joe slept on a rollaway, cramped in the farthest corner of the room. I slept well; Joe didn't. He still claims I tried to seduce him, and he dines out on the story at every opportunity. All Life Fitness guests now have their own rooms.

Joe was one of my rocks in the industry. The only other time we fell out was when I became frustrated by his inability to solve a problem that was probably unsolvable and I demanded to speak to the Life Fitness owner, Robert Maclure. Joe refused to get him.

"I want to speak to the organ grinder, not the monkey," I screamed into the phone.

Joe terminated the call and we didn't speak for weeks. I later apologised. I decided I owed Joe an upgrade, so forever after I called him "The Grinder".

Thankfully, after his retirement, Joe never became a presenter telling people how to buy equipment.

Lately, even IHRSA has succumbed to the world of mediocre advice. Once, the conference presenters were successful people who had "been there, done that" in their own business or profession. Now, it's full of organisations and people flogging products and equipment under the none-too-subtle guise of educating attendees.

I only take notice of people who can demonstrate they've been successful and profitable in their chosen fields. Just because they're good spruikers and can deliver funny lines doesn't make them worthy of your attention.

Beware of failed gym owners and other hangers-on charging you for advice. Steer your own course. Create your own destiny. You'll be far better off.

WORKOUT 20

DON'T
DITCH YOUR
AMBITION

By the end of 2012, Zap had not just conquered its home state with our "Fortress Tasmania" strategy; we were invincible – or so we thought – and ready to take on the rest of the world.

Julius Caesar crossed the Rubicon River – between Italy and Gaul – against orders in 49 BC. That sparked the Roman Civil War, but Caesar ended up becoming dictator. We had a similar decision to make, but it meant crossing a ditch – as we Tasmanians like to call Bass Strait. I didn't want to rule Australia; just Melbourne would do.

I had reached my goal of fifteen clubs during the year (the count was now sixteen); and profits were rolling in – much more than I'd ever dreamed of. From a loss of $37,000 in 2007/08 we had made a net profit of nearly $2,500,000 in 2011/12. Talk about rivers of gold... we were sweating dollars … or at least our members were.

Diamonds from dumbbells. Who would've thought? I basked in the glory of it all.

Gone were my bitter curses and obscenities about Club Silly Wanker, my grumblings about not having any money and my worries about being too old. I felt as though I could play footy again! My arthritic knees suddenly straightened as I floated along Sandy Bay Road and the beaches of Cremorne, nodding at fellow joggers with a smile and a wave.

But the complaints at Club Silly Wanker had intensified. "All you care about is Zap. You've forgotten us," the members moaned. The pool was even colder and the banana in pyjamas had lodged an official complaint to council about the spa noise. Instead of doing my worst Basil Fawlty meltdown impression (it has always worried me that people reckon I look like him, too) I just smiled and said, "Tut tut, we'll fix it soon. Thanks for bringing it to my attention." Then walked out the door to my adorable Zaps, where members fawned over me as if I was royalty. And I, King of Cardio, paraded like a peacock around the gym floor.

I did feel good. It wasn't only the money; we'd been able to bring fitness to all parts of the state at a reasonable price (still just $10.95 a week) and people could work out whenever and wherever they wanted. It was certainly better than pubs selling beer and pokies and, let's face it, a lot of misery.

The "swamp-the-home-state" plan had other benefits: members' keys fitted all doors, so there were no excuses for not working out as you travelled around the island. And our 24-hour competitors were non-existent; Anytime Fitness was still struggling with its sole Launceston club.

We even toyed with the idea of building Zaps in Malaysia. My journalist son, Marcus, was working for Qatari media outlet Al Jazeera in Kuala Lumpur, and I frequently visited him and his wife, Leah, and my granddaughters, Nellie and Molly (who was born in KL the same day the first Zap opened: 2 March 2009).

I teamed up with the Life Fitness agent in KL, Randy Bozeman, an American from Texas who also owned some full-service fitness clubs, and we looked at Malaysian shop–houses to figure out how we could convert them into 24-hour gyms. Many hours were spent over sumptuous meals of nasi lemak and beef rendang washed down with Tiger beer, plotting how we could turn KL into Zap Fortress Malaysia.

But there were problems, not the least being that credit cards were so easily available in KL that the default rate was around 30 to 40 per cent; and, as we relied on credit cards for our direct debits, that would mean massive rejections. As well, Randy, God bless him, a great bloke, was also very religious; nothing wrong with that, except he seemed to rely on the Good Lord to provide his living and, when it came to putting up his share of the capital needed to begin operations, his saviour went missing.

No, there was only one place to go: across the ditch, to the big smoke (or smog) of Melbourne.

I was excited. I had gone there in 1966 as a young footballer to play for Fitzroy in the then VFL, but I hadn't gone on with it, even though I'd sealed a place in the senior team. I now had a chance to make amends and succeed in a different way. And, as a proud Tasmanian, I'd always been irritated by the arrogant and tiresome two-headed and shagging-your-sister jokes – standard fun for pollution-choked Melburnians as they gazed out over their bike-strewn, poop-brown Yarra: their substitute for the glorious royal-blue River Derwent. Time for revenge.

Joe Marguccio, The Grinder, was always sending me photos of potential sites in Melbourne and urging Zap to get into the Victorian market. "There are five million people in Victoria, not 500,000 like in Tassie," he was fond of reminding me.

I knew Tassie as though it was my private island fiefdom but I had no idea about Melbourne. To me the suburbs were all like foreign lands, inhabited by coffee-swilling, focaccia-chomping natives.

The Grinder came up with a site in Blackburn. I had to check the map and see where the hell it was (16 kilometres east of the Melbourne

CBD). The premises were on the second floor of a modest development owned by an unpredictable German, Jürgen, and in a previous life it had been an average Chinese restaurant (and also a front for bikies selling drugs, I later learned).

Jürgen could not do enough for us when we visited: a generous contribution towards our fit-out, a long rent-free period, promises of this and that, and a what-else-do-you-need attitude.

As you will read in the next chapter, once a landlord appears generous, particularly in Melbourne, warning lights should flash, and you should get out of the building as quickly as possible. There's a reason they're being so compliant: it's a shit site and they're desperate to rent it to some sucker from Tassie.

The Grinder, born and bred in Melbourne (with Sicilian blood), was adamant the site was great: good car parking; proximity to a busy retail strip and railway station (why do you need trains? I'm from Tassie); and a great vibe.

Sorry Grinder, Blackburn was just short of disastrous. Apart from being tucked away from the mainstream, as soon as we signed the lease, Jürgen went feral. He refused to do half of what he promised, ignored building defects and – amid a string of obscenities – threatened eviction before we'd opened. His phone went dead whenever we requested help.

And then came Jürgen's finest moment. Unbeknown to us, although we should've done our homework and found out, directly below our gym was a hearing aid company. Yeah, you heard right, a hearing-aid company. They needed deathly silence to test clients' hearing. Silence: just what you'd expect from a gym.

Oh, how they loved the puffs and grunts and clanging weight stacks and dropped dumbbells and barbells that reverberated on the cracked concrete floor above them. "Can you hear anything, Sir?" they must've asked clients as they tested for the latest earpiece. "Yes, it's amazing. Thought I was deaf, but I can hear all this banging and crashing. Don't think I need a hearing aid now."

You've got to be careful about feeling over-confident, invincible and infallible. It's easy to get carried away.

The hearing-aid business rented about 80 square metres of space, and we had 500 square metres. So, as the complaints escalated at an alarming rate, we slept easy in the knowledge we'd have Jürgen's support; money speaks louder than a few dropped weights, right?

Wrong. Jürgen, of course, supported the hearing-aid company. Each week we received another threatening letter ordering us to do something about the noise. We were referred to our lease, which said our neighbours had to have "quiet enjoyment" of their premises. There was no enjoyment for Zap at Blackburn. The gym never made any money; we broke even at best.

Another good business lesson learned: you've got to be careful about feeling over-confident, invincible and infallible. It's easy to get carried away.

But at least we had staked our claim in Melbourne. And the best was yet to come.

THE LOONY LAND OF LANDLORDS

A s I've demonstrated, the terms of a property lease are critical for any business. The wrong location or the wrong deal can break you – and I certainly found that out in Melbourne.

It was a lot easier in Tassie. The ground-breaking Rosny Zap proved difficult only because it was a new concept, but I had the next fourteen planned. Knowing my Tassie landlords had enormous advantages, not least because I was never asked for a security bond (usually the equivalent of three to twelve months' rent up front) to cover non-payment of rent or "make-good" at the end of the lease. (Unscrupulous landlords find reasons not to return the bond by always "discovering" damage.) The Tassie landlords could also see the rise of Zap and were keen to get on board, knowing their rent would be paid on time every month.

I looked forward to the ritual lunches at the Black Buffalo Hotel with Emmanuel Kalis, by now one of my main landlords and a good friend. The ritual was always the same: we'd chomp and swill through loads of dips and meats and Greek wine and ouzo and then, amid invitations to stay at his villa on Crete and promises of bags of Pink Eyes (potatoes) from his farm at Sandford, the portly EK would strike.

Sometimes I was lucky to get out with both thumbs intact: EK drove a hard deal behind his beaming Greek bonhomie. But once the deal was done, he always stuck to his word and did what he said he'd do. You can't ask for more than that. We did fall out once – big time – and it threatened Zap's existence. But, as with a lot of ongoing business relationships, if you can weather the storm, the bond becomes stronger and the trust greater. As long as you do weather the storm.

EK purpose-built our fourth Zap at Kingston, a beachside suburb ten minutes south of Hobart's CBD. We were due to open in March 2010, one year after our first at Rosny. The deal was that I would pay $200 a square metre and the approximate area would be 500 square metres but the final floor size would be determined when construction was finished (sometimes EK's floor plans didn't work out). Construction was running behind schedule, and I was worried about our March opening date. (Dates are important in the fitness game: February–March and September–October are the optimum times to open.)

EK had an ageing partner called Jack, who acted as foreman on the project. A few days before the projected opening, with rubber floor tiles and equipment stacked high to the ceiling, I noticed Jack on his knees with a measuring tape.

"What are you up to, Jack?" I queried.

"Just measuring the final size of the gym," he said. Jack's tape rose and fell over the obstacles lining the floor like a Manhattan run-scoring chart for a one-day cricket match. There was no one at the other end of the tape either; it just snaked around as Jack tugged and pulled.

"Bit bigger than we thought: 530 square metres," Jack finally announced triumphantly as he scrambled to his feet. That meant

Beware of developers and landlords offering great deals. There's a reason: the site stinks and they can't get anyone else.

another 30 square metres x $200 = $6,000 a year for Zap to pay.

"Bullshit, Jack. You can't measure like that with all that stuff around. We'll have to do it later when it's cleared," I protested.

"You calling me a liar?" Jack challenged. "We have to get the measurement for the lease before you open."

At that moment EK's large Mercedes pulled up outside and he strode into the gym looking very ebullient. At the thought of more money, he sided with Jack.

"Jack is honest, Bobby. Are you saying he's dishonest?" he said, playing the questioning-the-integrity card again. A bitter row broke out. EK erupted.

"Do you want it or not?" he threatened.

All the equipment, flooring and fit-out items had arrived. I was stuffed if we didn't open, not to mention the hit to Zap's credibility. The heated argument continued. Workers stopped and stared. Then EK stormed back to his car, shouting, "That's it. I'll use the building for something else," and refused to take my phone calls.

They wouldn't measure again and wouldn't countenance an independent survey. We already had more than 400 members on pre-sale, so rather than enter into a bitter legal dispute in which, whatever happened, Zap would lose, we eventually compromised on the area by splitting the difference to 515 square metres.

Lesson learned: Make sure your lease is watertight from the start and don't leave any loose ends to the last minute.

I didn't easily forgive EK. Eventually we sorted out our differences over, yes, lunch at the Black Buffalo. I decided I needed him more than he needed me, and from that day on our business relationship strengthened. Zap Kingston eventually opened on time and became one of our most successful gyms.

Back to Melbourne. In Victoria, Zap was unknown – and so was I. There was little point going around saying, "Remember me? I was with Fitzroy in 1966." Or "you'll know me. I was in Tasmanian politics." (Never, ever, mention politics!) And being from Tassie was like saying you were from Tanzania, such was the interest.

Zap had had a big reality check with Blackburn, and our swagger had been replaced by a more subdued gait. If we were serious about success in Victoria we had to be based in Melbourne. Tassie was almost saturated and I could fly back regularly when needed. And staff members would have somewhere to stay when they came over the ditch. Meg made the move with me.

In late 2013, we rented a townhouse/office/storeroom in Caulfield North and became the only non-Jews in Waiora Road. That turned out to be fortuitous; the Jewish community would play a big part in our future success. For now, we still had a hit-or-miss mentality: we did no scientific demographic modelling and we didn't hire any population experts to discover the best areas for this rogue outfit. Incredibly, we still thought we were in Tassie, and we stupidly stuck to driving around a heaving, traffic-jammed metropolis of five million people trying to find sites.

The Grinder had seen a building in Flemington. The only thing I knew about that suburb was its famous racecourse. The site was a former medical centre on a busy highway, and we did our usual dozens of drive-by suss-outs, feeling like would-be hit-and-run killers. I expressed interest to the agent. He came back and said the owners wanted to meet me; and, by the way, bring all your latest financial reports, tax returns, and references. You mean no ouzo and Greek wine?

Meg and I were ushered in to an elaborate board room where four suited men sat around a large table looking very solemn. They were accountants and lawyers, and I felt as though I was being measured for a coffin by a firm of undertakers.

But our figures... our glorious figures. I smugly handed over our results and instantaneously the frozen faces melted into smiles. And when Rapid-Fire Robert took the stage, the deal was sealed. The owners turned out to be conservative, genteel and reliable. I just wonder how they would've been if I'd shown them the figures from Club Silly Wanker.

We didn't know it then, but our major mainland breakthrough was a phone call away. We had become friends with one of our Tassie landlords, Andrew Bendel, who lived in Melbourne. He called me one morning to say he'd been driving down Glenhuntly Road, in Elsternwick, and had seen an old video store for rent. It would make a good site, he said.

Where the hell is Glenhuntly Road? Only a ten-minute drive from our townhouse, it turned out. We jumped in the car ready for another drive-by suss-out. And I was blown away. This was the perfect location for any gym – fronting, as it did, a busy strip mall (as they're called in the United States), with dual entrances to a massive rear car park.

Excited, I immediately called the agent.

"You're from Tassie? Really? Sorry, what was your name again?" Then a pause. "There are already six gyms interested in the site, including that big American franchise Anytime Fitness. You're too late."

"Well, can you please tell the owner anyway?"

The agent gave no promises. He had his commission pocketed already. The next day I got a call.

"Look, the owner wants to meet you. Not sure why. But can you come down to his office straight away."

And so started a tremendous friendship with another great owner, Jack Hoppe. Jack was in the rag trade, was a prominent member of the Jewish community and therefore barracked for the AFL footy club the

Melbourne Demons. We got talking footy... and immediately a rapport was struck. Jack also liked our story: the Tassie battlers coming over the water to take on the mainland gyms. Two hours later, we walked out of his office with the promise that he'd get back to us after talking to his real estate agent. It had gone well. We high-fived in anticipation.

"Well, you weren't my recommendation," the agent said, "but Jack likes you both, so he's giving it to you."

Thanks, Jack, and thanks Andrew Bendel, our Jewish friends. You helped us penetrate the Yarra curtain.

Jack struck a hard bargain but, like EK, he always stuck to his word. The old Video Ezy store was in a bad state of repair – water damage and uneven floor containing some asbestos – and it required heaps of tenant improvements which we gladly agreed to. I would've done anything to get the site.

Zap Elsternwick became one of our most successful gyms, turning a consistent bottom-line profit of more than $500,000 a year. The high rent (25 per cent on our projected revenue) became only 10 per cent with increased turnover. The profit margin hit my target of 35 per cent.

More importantly, the Jewish community now trusted us. And this led to many more sites, including the Melbourne jewel in our crown: in Carlisle Street, Balaclava.

I fell for it: a landlord who offers to fit out your gym for free and virtually throws you the key to move in at no cost to your business. We had appointed a Melbourne manager, John Glancy, whom we nicknamed Glancy of the Overflow (because he attended a late-night callout to fix an overflowing toilet in one of the gyms) after the famous Banjo Patterson poem. Glancy was good at his job, and also one of those blokes who knew someone who knew someone whenever you wanted something done.

We'd flown Wayne Palmer and our team of Tassie contractors across to build the Blackburn and Flemington gyms. That was good for our Tassie image but became uneconomical, so we looked around for a Victorian firm. When we were looking to build another gym, at Carlton North, we found a fiery and fanatical Essendon-supporting builder whom we nicknamed The Bantam. Each small detail during the build had developed into a massive dispute, with The Bantam flapping around dangerously, threatening all sorts of revenge if we didn't do it his way. We soon left his barnyard.

Of course, Glancy had a mate who knew a mate. The mate worked for a building firm based in Mount Waverley. And from that contact came the alleged deal of a lifetime.

"They are developing a site at Braybrook and they're willing to do the fit-out free of charge," Glancy announced excitedly one day.

Everything?

"Yep, even pay for the flooring. All we'll need is equipment," Glancy gushed. "It's 700 square metres and the rent's only $100 per square metre."

Sound too good to be true? It was.

Braybrook, about 10 kilometres west of Melbourne, is – as I discovered to my horror when it was too late – one of the city's roughest suburbs. Burglary rates are high and it seemed to me that just surviving day to day without adding to the alarming murder rate was a challenge. Great place for a 24-hour gym!

When we drove out to look at the site the sun was shining and it didn't seem so bad. The building used to be the headquarters for legendary Aussie food manufacturer ETA. I remembered eating, as a kid, ETA peanut butter thickly spread on white toast with loads of freshly churned butter, and my keen sense of history was piqued. Hell, the building even had the original ETA sign dangling precariously from the roof.

Glancy was enthusiastic and the builders feted us like Roman soldiers returning home after another conquest, except it was the builders doing the conquering. There was already one forlorn furniture store in the complex, and they indicated prospective tenants were knocking down the doors of their headquarters to enter into the great deals they were offering. So we went ahead.

And we spent a fortune on equipment to fill the larger-than-usual floor space. But, hey, that's all we're paying for – right, Glancy?

I made the mistake of going out there one night before we opened. The streets were deserted, and I'm sure the locals, huddled behind shuttered windows, were wondering who was that idiot venturing out at night without an armoured car.

Glancy and the builders had "forgotten" that, tucked away around the corner, was a murderous body-building gym full of crazy, tattooed, steroid-filled meatheads, who proceeded to threaten anyone who joined Zap that it may be the last act they perform on this earth.

The builders also had another memory lapse when they didn't point out that the signage shown in their grand plans needed Heritage Council approval, which wasn't forthcoming. In the end, we were grateful because the roaming gangs had nothing to destroy or cover in graffiti, and the anonymity afforded by lack of signage meant no one joined. But at least the lone staff member who was courageous enough to work in the place survived. The membership peaked at 150 other courageous souls, all of whom deserved a bravery medal. And Zap experienced its first loss-making gym. The Zap Braybrook equipment is, to this day, in pristine condition – thanks to non-use, not good cleaning.

We debated whether we should close to cut our losses and quit but decided the stigma of shutting down would harm our brand in Melbourne.

Yes, it was my fault for not doing my homework better. But beware of developers and landlords offering great deals. There's a good reason: the site stinks and they can't get anyone else.

Probably the worst sort of landlord is the frustrating kind who won't return your phone calls when things go wrong. All over you to sign the lease, then they don't want to know you.

We experienced this at Williamstown. My Melbourne accountants had a client who owned a building in this lovely seaside suburb south-west of the CBD across Hobsons Bay. When the accountants knew we were looking in that area, they put us in touch with a wild-eyed, fuzzy-haired lawyer who, ominously, drove around in a Mercedes sports car.

His former tenant was the Commonwealth Bank. The CBA had come to the end of a long-term lease and, as we discovered later, couldn't wait to get out of there. The lease was far too expensive (as you'd expect when the bank had come to the end of a ten-year term with 4 per cent annual increases), but there weren't many gyms in the area and we were keen to crack "Willy", as the suburb is affectionately known.

We dubbed the landlord, Gyro, after an old Disney cartoon character from the 1950s – Gyro Gearloose, a quite loveable woolly-haired, mad inventor in the Donald Duck family. Unfortunately, Gyro didn't live up to the loveable, but he certainly was inventive, especially when it came to not spending any money on the building.

He agreed to move a badly located bank strongroom, but when he got the quote he reneged. Asbestos was found, but that wasn't his responsibility. Worst of all, the place leaked like a sieve – usually all over our expensive cardio equipment every time it rained. Poor old Glancy used to have to drive more than 40 kilometres from Rowville, where he lived, to Williamstown to vainly try to stop the leaks and clean up the overflow (there we go again).

Gyro instructed his secretary to say he wasn't there – especially after it rained. If we did manage to track him down, the response was the same: "The building is your problem, not mine."

"All we want is a dry building that doesn't leak," I protested.

Under pressure, and threats of not paying rent, Gyro finally devised a cunning plan. He commissioned an unreliable plumber to inspect the roof after it rained. By the time the "roofie" arrived – sometimes days later – the rain had always stopped, and his stock answer was, "I can't find the leak, so we'll have to wait till it rains again." This manoeuvre was foolproof: you'll never have to fix the roof because you're never there when it rains.

As far as I know the roof is still leaking. But Glancy isn't there, and, thankfully, nor am I.

In all of Zap's days, most landlords were excellent. They appreciated good long-term tenants, and wanted to keep them by fixing any building defects immediately. But the exceptions, such as Gyro, poured cold water – rainwater – on the reputation of landlords.

LEASE OF LIFE... OR DEATH

H ere are my rules for negotiating property leases (gained from many years of pain). My simple philosophy was: If you can walk away you'll get a good deal. In other words don't become too emotionally involved and don't want the deal so badly that you end up paying too much.

Rent ratio: Pay no more than 20 to 25 per cent of your projected revenue for annualised rent, including all outgoings. The optimum is 10 per cent of total revenue – and you can achieve that by beating projections or doing a red-hot deal.

Annual increases: No more than 3 per cent, or in these days of consistent low inflation, CPI. Most of our leases were 3 per cent or CPI – whichever is the greater. But I'd now be saying whichever is the lesser.

Outgoings: Try for a gross rent (landlord pays all property outgoings such as land tax, rates, water, body corporate fees). The

If you can walk away you'll get a good deal.

Retail Tenancy Act in Victoria legislates that landlords have to pay land tax. That's not the case in Tassie, where mostly tenants bear the brunt.

Leasehold improvements: Try to get the landlord to contribute towards your fit-out (I always tried for at least $50,000). Sometimes a landlord will do all the improvements in exchange for a higher rent; and you can claim the extra rent off your tax each year instead of depreciating the improvements.

Length of lease: If you can get a great deal in a great location, go for a ten-year lease with another two five-year options. But you must be sure it's a great deal and you can make it work before committing. The worst thing you can do is commit to ten years at, say, a 4 per cent annual increase, because by the tenth year you'll be paying 50 per cent more annually. And heaven forbid if your business goes broke.

Most common terms: Zap usually settled on a five-year lease with at least two five-year options.

Beware development clauses: Never, ever, take out a lease that contains a demolition, or development, clause. This means the owner can sell the property to a developer and boot you out after a few years. Just when you've slaved day and night to build up the business, you'll be out.

Market review: Be careful of market reviews. Unscrupulous landlords will get a valuer "mate" to jack up your rent at the end of your first lease term. Make sure you can get your own valuation. Victoria does not allow "ratchet" clauses (where the rent can't go below what is presently being paid), but Tassie does.

Know when your lease ends: It's very important to flag a reminder at least six months before your lease term expires, so you can start to negotiate with the landlord your options to renew. If you leave it until the last minute, the landlord can screw you.

Security bonds: Landlords will usually demand up to 12 months' rent as a security bond. The excuse is that it's a safeguard if your payments fall behind, or it will meet the cost of "making good" at the end of your lease term. This can be cash or in the form of a bank guarantee. Either way, it's a big impost. The problem is that most landlords usually find a way to keep some or most of it at the end. I never paid more than three months – and the average was two. Stare down your landlords on this – most will relent and be reasonable.

Take pictures: It's important to photograph all the interior improvements you make before you open for business – especially if they're substantial. I've had situations where the building had to be gutted and we did all the work to turn it into a schmick modern gym – only to have the landlord try to take credit for the work and use it in market reviews as reasons for extra rent.

Relationships: Try to establish good relations with your landlords; not all will take you out for a Greek ouzo lunch, but at least get their mobile number. It's much easier to call the owner direct if things go wrong than trying to go through property agents or difficult personal assistants.

Fine print: Always make sure your leases are subject to local government planning approval, and always add all statutory authority approvals to cover building and plumbing permits. Often you receive planning approval, but not the other permits. Landlords expect you to start paying rent even if you can't start the fit-out.

Avoid shopping centres: Don't get sucked into shopping centres. Rents are usually too high, and annual increases are 5 per cent or more. You have no location security, because landlords can move you around whenever they feel like it. Above all, gyms are not suited to big retail centres. Patrons go there to shop till they drop – not for a workout.

HOW NOT TO HIRE STAFF

I always had trouble hiring staff – or *the team*, as they have to be called in this politically correct world (but, whether you like it or not, they work *for you*, not *with you*).

So, the purpose of this workout is to give you my basic hiring tips, then tell you what I actually did – and advise you to do the opposite.

BOB'S TOP 10 HIRING TIPS
Don't Hire People Who:

1   have unexplainable gaps in their CVs
2   are currently doing uni degrees either full-time or part-time, or have another job
3   talk badly of their former boss (they'll do the same about you)
4   say they work smarter, not harder
5   say they left their other job because it was too stressful (And now they're working for me!)

6   have references from politicians

7   say they want job security (They have to earn it before they get it)

8   say they're doing it for the money

9   ask about holidays

10 have relations involved in the trade union movement.

My business career is littered with spectacular failures in vital positions that made running my businesses a lot harder. Often, they took up valuable time dealing with Fair Work Australia and claims for unfair dismissals and affirmative action, as well as all the rest of the workplace hand grenades. More of that later.

By now, you know the fitness industry is, well, different. It's unusual because most of the frontline staff do it because they love the job. Money is secondary; they get high on job satisfaction – helping people get fit and healthy and to live longer, more satisfying lives. That's hard to beat. Even commissions and bonuses don't really cut it. But recognition, a personal thank you and "well done" work wonders. All this is music to the ears for a bottom-line boss.

I love working with youngsters (most of our frontline gym staff were in their twenties); as an old bloke in his sixties they kept me young. And vigilant.

Zap gyms were staffed forty hours a week. So we usually had one person doing thirty-two hours and a back-up doing eight hours (normally Friday and Saturday). Initially, that person's main job was selling memberships and keeping the gym clean (dirt is death in the gym industry). Later, when we became the first gym in Australia to sell memberships online, their job was more about cleaning and walking around the gym talking to members.

Easy, eh? The problem was this: you needed back-up – so no one person could do forty hours. And thirty-two hours, and certainly eight hours, wasn't enough for a full-time job. Which meant uni students. Oh, dear.

Meg hired most of the frontline staff. I got involved with key positions because, after all, I had to work with them. We agonised over what to call the frontliners. We hated the usual "membership consultant", "membership manager" or even just "manager". But we had used "sales consultants" in our 2009 enterprise agreement – which was struck when we only had Club Silly Wanker – so that's what we were stuck with. (Meg eventually came up with the inspired "active-ists". More of that later.)

But uni students! It's got nothing to do with the fact that I failed Year 10. Honest. Uni-corns – as we called them – are great young people building the base for future stellar careers; but, let's face it, most of them are studying to be vets or accountants or lawyers or IT specialists; and they're going to change the world. But not my Zap world. With Zap there was a lot of autonomy – and downtime if you weren't a self-starter. You were virtually your own boss, which meant it was ideal for studying and doing uni assignments during Zap hours.

I begged Meg not to employ uni students, but her answer was always the same: Where else do we get part-time people?

My favourite trick was to zap into gyms without notice. Mostly the uni students were staring intently into our laptop computer, oblivious of anyone coming through the door. They looked up in horror to see me standing there with a reptilian smile. There was a panicked flurry of fingers on the keyboard, hurriedly exiting whatever was on the screen.

"Hi, Sarah. What are you doing?"

"Hi, Bob. Just checking last night's entries to see nobody got in without a membership," says Sarah smiling nervously but sweetly. "Ah, great. Can I have a look?"

As you move around to the other side of the desk you note the mound of newly minted paper from the printer with headings like "History of Ancient Rome" or "The Theory of Bipeds in the Kalahari Desert".

The laptop screen now has an innocent list of the latest Zap member entries but lurking in Recent History is a kaleidoscope of university-inspired assignments and research – all skulking under the proud Zap logo. Sarah sobs that she was behind in her university work and was going to take the day off but didn't want to let me down. I've always been a sucker for female tears, so she survives with a stern lecture.

In addition to helping people live longer and healthier lives, I now console myself with the fact that I have sponsored dozens of young people through university and enhanced the productivity of the nation. There was even one gym where the data download exceeded our limit by more than ten times: "Just researching gym equipment to see what's available to help you out, Bob," said history honours student James. Yeah, right, thanks so much!

The fact is, Zap almost ran itself. The sales assistants were really order takers. You didn't have to talk people into memberships, because the transparent price and unequalled facilities did the job for you. But the front desk "team" still needed to keep the place clean and walk around the gym talking to members. I insisted that every person be greeted and farewelled with at least the old standard "Bye. How was your workout?" or "When will we see you again?"

Nothing annoyed me more than staff glued to the laptop and ignoring people as they entered and departed. At least with Club Silly Wanker and Dockside there was forced interaction in the form of handing out towels and locker keys and checking in members on the computer.

(*Footnote:* One problem did occur at Dockside when one of our favourite members, Grace Alloca, waltzed up to a new front desk staffer to check in and announced, "Grace Alloca". Lockers were optional, and Grace came "hot to trot" in full gear, so she was somewhat bemused when she received a key anyway because our young recruit thought she had said "Grace, a locker.")

Initially, as mentioned, to force staff to stand and move around, I refused to supply seating behind the desk. But when occupational health and safety issues arose, I backed down and provided very uncomfortable chairs – the harder, the better.

I maintained the casual status of staff (paid more but no holidays), mainly because it was hard to get fill-ins when they wanted time off. My decision was reinforced when I relented and gave a key staff member

Zap almost ran itself. The sales assistants were really order takers. You didn't have to talk people into memberships.

at one of our biggest gyms permanent status so he could obtain a housing loan. He then proceeded to treat his two weeks' personal and sick leave like a piggy bank of days off. As soon as the month ended and he had another day's sick leave up his sleeve, he took the day off. He knew that, under our agreement, he needed a doctor's certificate only if he was off for two days or more.

"What was wrong with you, Jason?" Gastro or flu or migraine or constipation or toothache excuses flowed. He had no reason to tell me anyway; all you have to say under privacy laws is, "Medical condition, now bugger off, Bob."

I tried everything to hire good staff: "Who do you most admire in the world?" was a stock question I would ask.

"My father."

"Other than your father. Someone else."

"My grandmother."

"No, I mean, what about Nelson Mandela or Mahatma Gandhi or Winston Churchill?"

"Who are they?"

In desperation I went to recruitment agencies, which I found useless. They charge like wounded bulls and send you desperate people who make a living out of swindling business owners and recruitment executives.

My worst failing on the recruitment front was not having watertight position descriptions. I didn't want staff restricted by pages full of "do this" and "don't do that", so I issued parameters and thought everyone would be like me – creative and entrepreneurial within those boundaries. I wanted them to fly high. The problem is, there's room for only one entrepreneur in each business. To my great detriment, I found, entrepreneurs are not born to work for someone else. You need solid job descriptions, so staff don't step out of line. You need people who don't want to start their own business and just want a good job and to be looked after. And remember they're never going to work as hard as you do.

Then there was my final sneaky trick: the chair shuffle. This always took place after the first group interview (we had so many applicants that it became the norm to conduct initial "crowd" interviews before final one-on-ones). It went like this: You strategically place a cluster of chairs outside the interview room door. As the applicants are leaving you say something like, "See you later, guys (hate that Americanism, but can't say blokes), thanks for coming. Sorry, I just have to move these chairs into another room for a meeting." And you start picking up a chair as you speak. The theory is (I got this at an IHRSA conference), that, if one of the prospective employees helps you, they're showing initiative and will carry that into their Zap job.

Sadly, most left with a wave – or even in some cases making an obscene "bird" with middle finger, thankful to get out of the place and wondering why the hell that old bastard is shifting chairs around at his age? One of the few applicants who did help me with the chairs – and got the job on the strength of it – certainly showed initiative... by stealing the $580 cash she received for an upfront membership. After that we only dealt in fortnightly direct debits and the chair trick was eventually abandoned.

Meg also became tired of constant group interviews and thought she would try something different: Zumba classes. I remember driving up to the Moonah Zap one day in 2013 and being staggered to see a group of at least 30 people dancing in the car park to Zumba music.

Just as I screeched to a halt in the street (couldn't fit in the car park), ready to ask what the hell was going on, I noticed Meg at the head of the tone-deaf rabble, happily Zumba-ing away.

"Just seeing how they work together as a team," was her explanation.

And then there was Douglas. My worst effort, by far. By 2014, with our rapid expansion and move to Melbourne, I was struggling to keep all the balls in the air. Meg was officially group sales and marketing manager, but she liked to be referred to as CEO, which in fact she was. I labelled myself the Rupert Murdoch–like executive chairman (mainly so I could eventually retire and still be chairman). We needed a hard-working, savvy Tasmanian state manager to oversee our Fortress Tasmania operations. And again we realised that, due to the uniqueness of the health-and-fitness industry, it was hard to bring in an "outsider" who didn't understand the nuances of the gym game. Big mistake: in my experience the gym industry seems to attract people with serious issues and hidden personality disorders.

Douglas came highly recommended by industry colleagues. Meg also knew him – and his wife – and had worked with him at a Melbourne gym chain many moons before. I was so desperate to find someone who knew the industry that I didn't even bother asking for references. Also, there were gaps in his CV – like working overseas for a time – and he'd been "consulting" to rather strange organisations, which he managed to explain away, as most conmen do.

Douglas was old for the industry – in his late fifties – but, hey, as a just-turned septuagenarian myself, who was I to talk? And over several dinners and meetings he showed he knew the gym lingo. Some concerns arose when we had a group brainstorming session with a Melbourne advertising agency to find a new slogan – and Douglas made the remark that staff were more important than profits. (I had the feeling this was coming from a place of self-interest, not altruism.) But on we went, and Douglas prepared to move to Tassie to head up our operations.

Part of the deal was that I would pay for the rent on a house for

Douglas and his wife. He started to look, but vacancies were few. My holiday house was free, and I wanted to show our new man how much we wanted him to succeed.

"Tell you what, you can live in my beach house until you find somewhere to stay," I offered.

Douglas ("Don't call me Doug") jumped at the chance. And with golden sands and gentle waves lapping at his front door, he never wanted to leave.

As I pursued our Zap dreams interstate, I became increasingly worried about the eccentric Douglas, with reports filtering back that he was using out-of-date, twenty-year-old sales systems ("borrowed" from another fitness chain) and getting around our gyms at the height of summer in a double-breasted navy reefer jacket and cravat. Not exactly the gear to relate to twenty-something staff in red T-shirts and track pants. I phoned him to say that maybe a more relaxed dress style might be a good idea.

Worry increased to alarm as he started to tell staff he was going to change our success formula by introducing all the anachronisms I had just turfed out. I spoke to several key staff members and they reckoned he was "a joke".

I decided enough was enough, and I phoned Douglas to say I was flying to Hobart the next day and wanted to set up a meeting. My intention was to sack him as his probationary period was still in play. Unfortunately, I'd confided my intentions to another key staff member, and I strongly suspect he warned Douglas about his fate.

As I boarded the plane to Tassie, I received a hysterical phone call from a receptionist in our Salamanca headquarters to say there'd been a terrible accident: Douglas had fallen head first down the stairs leading to our basement – and had suffered serious injuries. Sure enough, Douglas had apparently tripped on a suspicious looking carpet tear, tumbled down the stairs – or slid down as my surprised financial controller later described it – and ended up slumped in front of the desk.

With no thought of coming back to work, Douglas spent the next few weeks going to assorted doctors and specialists with various life-threatening complaints – all at my expense and none of which showed any real damage. To make matters worse, he was still living in my holiday home at Cremorne.

Christmas was looming and Stephanie and I had arranged a traditional family gathering at Cremorne. I sought a meeting with Douglas.

"You'll need to move out of Cremorne by Christmas," I said as gently as I could. "I need my house. My family are coming home."

He refused, and accused me of harassment.

"For Christ sake, it's my bloody house, and I only let you in there out of the goodness of my heart."

Douglas proceeded to sue me for everything you can think of. In the end it cost my company nearly $50,000 to get rid of Douglas – and for me to get my house back. When our family eventually moved in, there was plenty of damage and items were missing. But at least I had my holiday home for Christmas.

All of this happened because I didn't do my homework properly and relied on goodwill rather than good sense.

So please read the above again… and do the opposite of what I did.

ROIDS RAGE IS A REAL PRICK

It's confession time again. And I've been trying to avoid the subject.

Steroids: unfortunately, for personal trainers and many members, they ARE the industry.

I'd like to say my gyms were clean of steroids (known in gymland as Roids) but I have to admit, hard as I tried to eradicate the menace, modern gyms are awash with the stuff. It's a sad truth. If you drool over a celebrity's picture and admire their abs, butt, biceps or rig, and believe fortune has bestowed them with an elite composition of flesh, you've been conned. They're more likely to be on the Roids.

But the thought of perfection keeps members coming back, doesn't it? They're close but not quite there. Another training session perhaps? Carb cycling, fasting, kilojoule counting, more heavy reps, load that protein. Never mind genetics, never mind whether their body type is ectomorph, mesomorph or endomorph. They believe that if they just

lift a few more kilos, deny hunger, or eat more, interval train, mix some more creatine and weigh that chicken breast they will have success. Oh, yeah, and meditate too.

But it's all bullshit. Without the Roids they are highly unlikely to look like the perfect poseur on the front of a fitness mag.

Steroids are synthetically produced testosterone which, when injected or taken orally, can dramatically increase muscle mass in a very short time. Men were once more likely than women to be on them – but these days females want to look ripped, too. Steroids are illegal in Australia but are readily available on the internet and easy to pick up cheaply in South-East Asia and from underground labs. And, I hate to say it, from gym members and trainers. At one time, I could look around my gyms and find stashes everywhere. I discovered them in toilet cisterns, shower bays, desk drawers and ceiling tiles, and under treadmills. All left for collection by users or dealers. Some police I know reckon the steroid game is larger than the illicit drug caper. I doubt that, but it's a huge trade all over Australia – and Tassie is no exception. We often called the police, but arrests were few.

Gyms have become the province of young people looking to socialise (80 per cent of Zap members were under forty and 60 per cent under thirty). They link up with their friends and chat, take pics of their bodies for Instagram, laugh and joke and, just occasionally, work out. So, it's no wonder they're trying to look better than anyone else; it's competitive. Developing muscle is hard work and a bit of help is welcome.

In my young days, the place to socialise was the pub, where we'd meet up over a beer or two. If you wanted to look great, you'd cover your body with good clobber. In the modern meeting place – the gym – you're virtually naked, and your body is your image. No place for sickly, thin or fat, out-of-shape flesh. I feel sorry for today's youth. In these days of body image at all costs, members can get no further than a certain stage of development without some help from artificial stimulants. The temptation to achieve the perfect body, ripped and rippling with glistening muscle, is strong.

I remember back in the days of Lifestyle, before it became Dockside, manager Waxo had a meathead bodybuilder named Clarrie, who used to accompany him on dangerous trips – like to banks, to ask for equipment finance or loans, or to landlords to talk about rent arrears. Clarrie boasted the proud title of Mr Tasmania – and flew in Waxo's Cessna aircraft to compete in Mr Australia contests. Clarrie was likeable but so muscle-bound and grotesque that he could hardly walk without assistance. Goodness knows how the plane got off the runway. He was on Waxo's payroll, but he spent most of his working time desk-bound, sucking on protein concoctions and injecting Roids (which were first created in 1935) into his porcupine skin while, for the 200th time, watching Arnold Schwarzenegger in the movie *Pumping Iron*. Sadly, he died from heart failure in his thirties – plaque build-up being one of the many side effects of this fearsome drug, which plays around with hormone balance.

All of which gets me to the point about personal trainers, or PTs. They were my biggest nightmare in the gym industry: hard to handle, moody, aggressive volatile beasts. And all because of the Roids. I'd say 80 per cent of PTs take steroids. Just ask to see your PT's glutes or quads – if they're covered in boils from the needle pricks, they're definitely on the Roids.

The habit has almost become a value-add for personal trainers – like a set of steak knives for a course of ten sessions. PT training institutions, most receiving government funding, are potentially churning out drug mules. Roids delivered to the gyms – commission on sales – sessions based on Roids. Simple. Once I intercepted the delivery of a box of syringes for collection by a PT. I was tipped off by a fellow PT who ratted on his mate because he was clean himself and had lost a family member to Roids and cocaine. Of course, I sacked the guilty PT. But did I get accolades for attempting to run clean gyms? No. I was abused by two members – obviously the would-be recipients. "Why did you sack him? Everyone's on the Roids." Not in my gyms.

One PT, who was always short of money, went from garden

gnome to Robo-Cop in about six weeks. Unfortunately, just before a bodybuilding competition, he developed equine flu – because he'd used a cheap, and legal, strain of Roids often administered to horses.

Another country boy, whom I'd personally mentored when he started with Zap, went feral while I was away and, after trying and failing for three years, developed an Arnie body almost overnight. I was sent photos of the kid on stage in a competition – orange from spray tan and looking dehydrated, skeletal, small-waisted, and yet massive. Must be the country air, eh? An investigation discovered that he'd been silly enough to order Roids from the dark web on his work computer. Once a country boy, always a country boy – and he no doubt enjoyed the green pastures after his dismissal.

As mentioned, females aren't exempt from the Roids scourge. It's all about gender equality nowadays – do what the boys do, and even hold our own fitness competitions. Muscular, toned, shapely bodies glistening with baby oil teeter, in heels, on mirrored big-barn stages – lured by the promise of winning, and getting onto front covers and Instagram and all that.

Another female PT, who specialised in training her Zap colleagues for the big comps, called me aside one day and earnestly explained that when girls get really lean and ripped their menstrual cycle stops, so I needed to be understanding if they couldn't concentrate, email or clean the gym because the event was only a few days away. But that's not all. I also had to turn a blind eye to what was happening under the desks: protein shakes, containers of pills, hidden needles, and heavy use of particular internet sites. Apparently, staff parties were full of rude – I mean Roid – talk of shrunken testicles and protruding labials. Thankfully, I'd always gone home before party time.

I once had a gym session with a recently hired PT who was very good at his job. Afterwards, to thank (and pay) him, I walked with him to his car. That was when he accidentally dropped his rather large sports bag – and out cascaded a waterfall of syringes. I paid him and sacked him at the same time.

Personal trainers were my biggest nightmare... hard to handle, moody, aggressive volatile beasts.

Roids are highly addictive. One day a PT is a nice bloke; the next an aggressive, threatening monster as the drug kicks in. I've lost count of the number of times I've come to fisticuffs in the office with a normally gentle PT who suddenly turned into Mike Tyson. The worst times are when the annual state bodybuilding championships loom. Suddenly, within a few weeks, triathlete-bodied, arrow-shaped PTs become Incredible Hulks, with an attitude to match. In my gyms, clients often walked out in disgust; disputes became frequent.

Acting on experience, I insisted Zap PTs were not directly employed; they were to be independent contractors running their own business on licence in our gyms – a business within a business, like lions renting a game park. If they had attitude, they could take it out on their prey – I mean clients – not me. They paid Zap a weekly rent of $220; and they made their own appointments and kept all the fees they charged. But still there were problems. After all, they were PTs.

I asked that they all wear Zap T-shirts with PERSONAL TRAINER emblazoned on the back (issued free of charge) to protect our brand (sometimes with regret when Mike Tyson reappeared in one in the run-up to bodybuilding titles). They'd often straggle in wearing trackies and daggy flannels that they had obviously slept in the previous night. I'd get a call from a dedicated front desk staffer dobbing them in. And then all hell would break loose as I gave her permission to tell him, "Go change or else."

PTs would also try to recruit our members for private outdoor boot camps, to train in their house garage and flog supplements, and Roids. But, with more than fifty PTs, you couldn't microchip them all. And then there was the other extreme: the PTs who weren't on the Roids but were also slightly peculiar. One, Jerry, insisted on eating twelve rounds of toast and honey just before every training session. There were no real benefits, but he insisted on doing it anyway. At Zap meetings, he'd drop to the floor and start doing fifty push-ups just as the presenter was making an important point. The other attendees would stare in disbelief. Sometimes I wished he was on the Roids.

I never wanted Zap to be for bodybuilders. They tie up equipment for hours on end as they do multiple sets, and they jealously guard the bench and weights in between. They wear Chesty Bond singlets to show off their tattooed biceps and sweat like pigs. Big turn-off for most members, especially women.

We had one Moonah thug nicknamed Arnie (yes, after THE Arnie), built like a brick shithouse, who would go crazy and start fights with anyone who dared to question his authority. Members were leaving in droves because of Arnie. I had to get rid of him but nobody was game to front him and tell him his fate. Finally, Dr Strangelove, who was now working for us full-time, volunteered to do it by phone. Arnie cursed and swore and vowed revenge on Zap, but the good doctor quickly cut off his Zapper key.

Next day we learned of Arnie's revenge. He let it be known that he'd gone and joined our competitor Anytime Fitness, even though they were 10 kilometres from his home. That would teach us, thought the Roids-dumb Arnie. I couldn't stop laughing. Revenge on whom? He was soon begging to come back; but, no, sorry Arnie, you and Anytime deserved each other.

Deliberately, I restricted our dumbbell sets to a maximum of 40 kilograms (bodybuilders want 60 kilogram-plus dumbbells) and supplied minimum heavy-duty equipment. But I forgot that these misshapen gorillas love performing for an audience, preferably female, and Zap was the ideal gym for that.

Initially, I made the mistake of giving selected non-Roids PTs some desk hours as well, to supplement their income. Invariably, they'd use their desk time to also train clients or would start twenty minutes late because their morning PT session went over time. That idea was soon abandoned.

Roids can cause depression. So, after the annual bodybuilding championships, and invariably little or no success, sulking and skulking would replace rage. Poor clients. Roids are supposed to enhance self-esteem but PTs never lacked that in the first place. So why do they do it? They're sold on emotion and playing on self-esteem. But obsession leads to addiction.

If Roids use was legal, I could have doubled my profits. But I didn't need Roids. And nor do you.

So, if you're ever about to hire a PT – and there are some excellent ones around who can really enhance a gym business – just ask them to turn around and drop their pants so you can check for boils and needle marks.

I'm sure they won't mind. Unless it's just before a major comp.

THE MONEY-GRABBING MADDIES

Marketing and promotion of your product are very important in the fitness business. But beware the Mad Men from advertising agencies.

I refer, of course, to the excellent TV series *Mad Men*, based on a New York advertising agency in the 1960s. Little has changed since then, except women now share the board table. For the sake of gender equality, I'll refer to the Mad Men as the Maddies. They'll still screw you and take all your money; the bigger the agency, the bigger the bill.

I've found that I can come up with better ideas, write better copy and save myself a lot of cash. And you can too, as already mentioned. Just grab yourself a good graphic designer to consummate your own creativity. They can do your logo and website, which are critical in promoting your business. I wrote my own copy, but you can always hire a copywriter for around $50 an hour.

What has changed since the 1960s is that we now live in a world of digital marketing. Zap, for example, became a media company selling fitness.

When I owned Dockside, I used to spend about 5 per cent of revenue on advertising. In the 1980s and 90s, television was king, usually backed up by newspapers and direct mail. It was advertise or die: the halcyon days. And didn't we all love seeing our gyms on TV? And using the members and staff (with their permission of course) as extras lolling about on treadmills and in pools; the mandatory close-up of pedalling feet and fluffy towels, and all the rest.

The only decent advertising agency I've dealt with in my nearly forty years in the gym game was a local crowd called EOAO – which stood for Every One An Original (the terrible name did nearly scare me off). Tragically, they no longer exist, but the principals still do.

EOAO was run by two blokes called Mark Grey and Russell Naughton, with Jock Chalmers producing our TV ads. Russell had been a top creative talent in Sydney before dropping out to the slower pace of Hobart, and we hit it off straight away, coming up with some great campaigns for Dockside and Club Silly Wanker (Russell now heads up a Sydney agency called Sliced Bread).

We won a national direct mail award for launching Silly Wanker in 1995 by sending out a steel pipe with the slogan "Look What's in the Pipeline". I cringe now to think how corny it was. Hell, we even got that old rocker Normie Rowe to open the place (little did he know he was unveiling a loss-making fitness leviathan). And I was able to capitalise on my love of sport when Dockside sponsored state cricket, football, the Tassie Devils basketball team – just about everything really. I enjoyed yarning with Warnie, Mark Taylor, Glenn McGrath and Allan Border when the Aussie Test team trained in the gym before Tests at Bellerive Oval. Warnie never minded me getting in his ear for hours at a time; he was just a knockabout kid breaking into the big time. Later,

Zap sponsored the Hobart Hurricanes, before the Big Bash took off and costs quadrupled overnight.

EOAO even did my political campaign free of charge. They had me, in suit and tie and carrying a briefcase, running behind a trailer (with a cameraman desperately hanging on), chanting, between pants, "I'm Bob Cheek, and I'm running for Denison." Corny again, but it worked: I won the seat for the Liberals.

Then came Zap and everything changed dramatically. Our budget for our first gym was $10,000, which included a direct mail drop and very minimal local newspaper ads. Traffic was driven by word of mouth and we lured people to our website by plastering the web address all over our buildings. Zap really sold itself by generating excitement because it was different. In Tassie, once we'd done the Rosny gym, the rest was relatively easy.

Finally, there was the advent of digital marketing, and Facebook; and advertising just got cheaper all over again.

The biggest breakthrough came when we perfected the concept of joining online. We had looked at outdoor kiosks attached to our gyms where members could join twenty-four hours a day, but there were problems with security. Because our competitors were franchise operations with different owners, they had difficulty joining members online, and we wanted to capitalise on their constraints. We asked Dr Strangelove and the Freak Factory to work their magic.

This they did. I received a call about 2am from the good Doctor to say he'd done it. And he certainly had. Suddenly, new members could join any time of the day or night. They paid the key fee and signed up for a fortnightly direct debit; all they had to do was call in and pick up their key from the club when they wanted to start. We literally made money while we slept.

Initially about 25 per cent of our members joined online – but this quickly rose to 40 per cent and eventually we had more members joining this way than we had calling in to the gyms. It was only possible because we had built such an outstanding reputation for quality in all our gyms, and prospective members didn't need to inspect. Every Zap was a carbon copy: same equipment, same layout, same wet areas, same cleanliness and service.

Later, Meg revolutionised the selling system by letting each gym staffer have their own Facebook page to communicate with leads and get prospects in to sign up. It was risky, because lazy employees could while away their time on Facebook without worrying about memberships. To overcome this, we decided on a controversial change to the staffers' job titles. This was when, instead of being known as sales consultants, they became "active-ists". And active they were. Almost without exception they treated each gym like their own franchised business with their own online service page. And sales boomed even more.

When we first moved to Melbourne as an unknown business, I was foolishly tempted to give advertising agencies one last try. I didn't know anyone, business and living costs were prohibitive and we had to build profile in a city of nearly five million people.

We'd just taken on new accountants in Melbourne and they recommended a second-tier agency headquartered in the suburb of Richmond.

"They do amazing work," our accountant gushed.

It was the same old story: attractive female account executive and a trendy male director wining and dining us in boardrooms and expensive restaurants around town; promising us the world, before handballing us to their struggling graphic designers and copywriters sitting behind partitions in a freezing, dark, dank corner of a restored warehouse. We just had to put up $15,000 for the initial "concept" session, another $15,000 for them to survey our clubs (plus expenses to Tasmania), $20,000 for an all-day "brainstorm" to find a new slogan... and on it went.

I had the idea that Zap should be marketed like Richard Branson's Virgin (challenging bloated and established parts of the business world with a cheaper and better model – be it music, airlines, trains, credit cards, islands or gyms). We were the challengers from Tassie – taking on the established and complacent mainland gym scene; the Tassie whitebait versus the Victorian Great Whites. At first, the frontline peddlers of perfection didn't like the idea because they didn't think of it. But when they saw I was convinced this was the way to go – and not wanting to lose an inbred colonial sponge they could squeeze for several months – they switched tack and became supportive.

Much to their horror, I declined all the money-making upfront padding on offer and persuaded them that we didn't need a new logo or branding, just ideas for tackling the big smoke (sorry, smog). But I did stupidly agree to a reduced-price, all-day session to come up with a new slogan. I thought our previous catchphrase, "Work out day and night", had become redundant as 24-hour gyms began to sweep the nation. Massive mistake.

Meg and I assembled a motley, Tasmanian best-available-at-the-time Zap crew for the Richmond day session and flew them to Melbourne at great expense. The entourage included Douglas, Glancy of the Overflow, Dr Strangelove and our new Tassie sales manager, Caitlin, who became so stressed she resigned when the session ended. For the uninitiated, this is what happens in these "brainstorming" sessions: the agency has a meeting the night before and decides what the slogan is going to be. Why? Because they know it's impossible to get a roomful of arguing imbeciles to agree on anything, let alone a slogan. In our case they happened to be right.

The meeting raged on all day with much volume but very little sense coming from anyone. Dr Strangelove was the exception – he sat all day in some sort of spell and didn't utter a word for the entire eight hours. Douglas made his aforementioned faux pas by raving on about staff being more important than profits – loved that angle; Glancy overflowed with love for the industry; and Caitlin used the occasion to settle old scores about not getting a pay rise.

About 3pm, the Richmond "moderator" had had enough and started to move the raging rabble towards the pre-ordained slogan. Now there is an art in this: the essence being to let the group believe they thought of it themselves, rather than having been manipulated into it.

"Now we're improving people's lives, right?" the manipulator–moderator shouted above the din. "And Zap is like a charge: Pow! Pow!" he screamed. Pandemonium broke out again, but he continued shouting in his high-pitched soprano: "Pow, pow, pow!"... until he triumphantly scribbled on the whiteboard, "Zap: Charge Your Life".

There was silence: Geez, did we really think of that?

"Well done guys (you must throw in plenty of "guys" if you're in advertising) that's incredible you came up with that," the manipulator hurriedly concluded. "I love it. Inspirational. Well done."

I didn't particularly like a slogan with "charge" in it – the connotation being we're going to hike prices – but I was so exhausted I agreed, and so did the warring troops, who wanted the free beer I'd promised back at their hotel.

The Richmond Maddies wasted no time in getting a photo of us all grouped around the whiteboard pointing to the unfortunate slogan (which was beginning to look worse by the minute) in case we changed our mind.

We did. It was never used. And the next day I loathed it, not least because the piece of crap had cost me $12,000.

The Maddies then turned to the creative part: coming up with the enlightened advertising that was going to see the island gym challengers rip apart the large, arrogant Melbourne chains and the hapless rest. First, of course, I had to sign a contract, paying so much a month for all the goodies and promises that awaited us. In other words, I was completely stitched up.

So, with the Maddies' mission accomplished, we waited. And waited. Finally, days later, we were called in for the masterpieces to be unveiled.

I was shocked: I had never seen worse advertising ideas. We were offered throwbacks to the 1970s, with pictures of big-breasted women in leotards, or even wedding dresses, lifting dumbbells; and muscular, tattooed Joe Palooka men with ripped singlets. All concocted by

I was shocked. I had never seen worse advertising ideas. We were offered throwbacks to the 1970s.

someone with no idea about the fitness industry regurgitating all the stereotyped, hideous images I'd worked for forty years to eradicate. As well, there were meaningless headlines like "Zap Fit: no counter-fits".

"What does that mean?" I countered.

"It's a play on 'no counterfeits'. You know, copying you," the advertising guru explained slowly to the colonials, as though we didn't comprehend pure genius.

"What about the Tassie challenger idea we agreed on?" I spat.

"The creative team didn't think that would work," he explained. "They know best."

Sorry Dad (only cowards lose their temper), but I exploded. I knocked the glossy A3 sheets off the table, rammed back my chair, and stormed out – with Meg trotting behind like an obedient Labrador. The by-now-panicked sales director lumbered alongside, blurting out, "We can do them again if you don't like them. For another fee, of course."

I kept going. Now the threats – "You've signed a contract" – echoed behind. The once sickeningly friendly company director turned ugly and went to his lawyer. Eventually we settled out of court. It was worth the money to escape their clutches.

Never again. No, you don't need the money-grabbing Maddies. Just do it yourself – with a little help from your friends the reasonably priced independent contractors.

And I also discovered I needed a new accountant – one of the Richmond Maddies was his brother-in-law.

LEARN TO LIGHTEN THE LOAD

Business can be intense. So it's important to have some fun, and lighten the load.

Meg and I found the best way was to come up with a name for every person we met – usually an animal or movie character as in the many examples you have already read. After all, nicknames are one of the great Aussie traditions. The only difference is that we kept ours to ourselves – until now.

They say most dog owners end up looking like their dogs, but it's also amazing how most people actually look like animals they don't own. And it's fun trying to find the creature that best describes them, or even just a moniker that rolls off the tongue better than their name. I don't mean the usual Aussie shorteners like Baz for Barry, or adding

Sitting opposite Richard, and thinking Python, relieved any stress.

S on the end of Langer for Langers; or Y on the tail of, well, Cheek for Cheeky; and the more common, lazy abbreviating of anything longer than eight or nine letters – like Adders for Addington. No, these were real characterisations – in our minds anyway. Not derogatory, just funny. Not meant to insult, just a way for us to release the pressure. If this all sounds juvenile and unbusinesslike, you're probably right. But it got us through many long days and nights.

If we had an important meeting or phone conversation, it was easier to wake up and say, "Today we've got to meet The Python" (our name for one particular property owner who we reckoned swallowed more than he could chew). That would usually bring a smile, instead of "Shit, we have to go through another session with Richard today."

Sitting opposite Richard, and thinking Python, relieved any stress and brought a wry smile every time he pontificated about his importance. As did meeting a new person and thinking of a name – often scribbled on a note passed to each other across the table. Mostly we contained our laughter.

As mentioned previously, there were the Bantams – small, fiery, flapping, antagonists. We had four of those: Original Bantam (our first Melbourne builder); Sea Bantam (charter skipper); Bible Bantam (a very religious employee) and Bullshit Bantam (a notorious fast-talking equipment salesman).

There were our key employees: Glancy of the Overflow and Dr Strangelove (both of whom you've already met); the Golden Greek (who is coming up); Miss Muffett; the Grinder; the Hamster; and Moonface. Some of our landlords were The Strangler, Shrek, Coyote, Gyro Gearloose and The Whippet. We even had names for ourselves: Meg was The Afghan, shortened to Affie, because of her unruly hair and uncanny ability to sniff out good sites; and I was the Monkey Warlord, abbreviated to MWL (because I sat on top of the tree and snarled at any intruders; and I've since learned my birth year is the Chinese year of the monkey, so that's a double fit!).

The only time we ever got caught out was when Meg, a great amateur cartoonist, was at a restaurant and couldn't resist the paper tablecloths and crayons (meant for kids). She did a great caricature of an acquaintance – complete with witty caption – photographed it and texted it to a friend... who then sent it to the subject involved. Accidentally of course!

This book mostly uses our self-made monikers, rather than real names. But because of situations and positions, it's inevitable people will recognise themselves as part of the story. Or think they do.

So, please don't take offence; just be happy that it helped us survive the fitness industry.

THE ART OF PALM-TREE MANAGEMENT

I was twenty-three when I bought my first business with my wife, Stephanie, who was two years younger. It was a run-down newsagency in the tiny, rain-lashed town of Penguin on Tassie's north-west coast. We had no money, but I talked my Dad into going guarantor for a bank loan ("Dad, I need to keep pedalling"). We worked bloody hard. I had a day job as a stock agent and afternoon and weekend employment as a footy coach and player. The rest of the time I joined Steph in the newsagency, selling everything from magazines to football boots and Matchbox toys. And delivering daily newspapers at 5am.

Ever since then, I had dreamed of owning a business where you didn't have to be at the "coalface" twelve hours a day and you could take time off and still have the business make money. After almost fifty years of hard labour, and PhD and MBA qualifications from my own School of Hard Knocks, that time had finally come.

At the beginning of 2015, I was nearly seventy-one and Zap was booming. Our net profit was almost $4 million and our EBITDA (earnings before interest, tax, depreciation and amortisation) was approaching $6 million. We had opened eight Zaps the previous year (that's one every six weeks), bringing our total to twenty-nine.

How things had changed for me... from a desperate, depressed, single-gym pauper to fitness empire guru in just six years. No worries about super now.

I was feeling – well – invincible. Time to enjoy life. And prove that Zap can run without its founder and chairman micro-managing every detail as though it was his private fiefdom.

I've always been a cricket tragic – from the time I built that indoor cricket centre in the 1980s, and had the likes of Dennis Lillee come to visit; to owning Dockside gym and yarning with Warnie and the rest; and hosting Ricky Ponting and the immortal teams of that era who worked out at Club Silly Wanker before Bellerive Tests.

When I was a kid in the 1950s, I used to lie in bed on frosty Tasmanian winter nights listening, on a crackling crystal set radio, to the dulcet tones of the BBC's John Arlott, picturing Lindsay Hassett, Neil Harvey and Ray Lindwall pummelling the Poms as they toured the famous English grounds: Lord's, The Oval, Old Trafford, Headingley, Edgbaston and Trent Bridge. I yearned to do the same thing – as a player. But lack of ability got in the way and this was my chance to at least fulfil my dream as a spectator, because the Aussies were off to England to try to retain the Ashes won the previous home summer. And, as another bonus, the Aussies were playing two Tests in the West Indies in May as a warm-up: just the excuse I needed to indulge in another fantasy of skippering a boat around the Caribbean. There was a small problem with that last ambition: I couldn't sail. My only experience on yachts was of being sprawled in the cabin drinking all the owner's booze while he battled a heavy swell on Hobart's River Derwent.

But, hey, I owned Zap and I was invincible wasn't I?

In April 2015, Meg and I hopped on a plane to New York and then the Caribbean via Miami. I had appointed Glancy of the Overflow as acting CEO, supported by Dr Strangelove in Tassie, and the Golden Greek, Greg Kassidas, in Melbourne. It was a risk, but at least none of them had resigned when offered the job, which was encouraging. I think they were more excited to have the boss overseas than I was.

Due to evolving technology, Zap just about ran itself and there was no longer the tyranny of distance. I could now pay the bills and payroll, and transfer funds, while sitting under a palm tree in Barbados, Jamaica or Antigua – a damn sight better than a cold, windowless room in the bowels of Salamanca Mews.

I discovered a small sailing school – LTD Sailing – in an exotic and remote location on the tiny Caribbean island of Grenada, famous for its nutmeg and known as the Spice Island after Ronald Reagan sent US troops to invade this diminutive nation in 1983. The school was run by a young American couple – Chris and Chrystal Rundlett – and they were offering two-week courses sailing among the Grenadines, an incredibly beautiful necklace of islands north of Grenada. At the end, if you passed, you would get an American Sailing Association skipper's certificate enabling you to charter and sail a catamaran. In my case, in the unlikely event I passed, it was like being handed a licence to drown.

The Rundletts returned my email with astonishment: "You can get sailing courses in the Whitsundays, you know," said Chris. "That would save you a lot of money."

"After I get my skipper's licence I want to sail to Dominica for the first Test and then Jamaica for the second," I enthused.

Silence.

"You do realise that's 1,200 miles away?"

No, I hadn't.

The Rundletts were no romantics of the high seas. I'm not sure if they thought training a 71-year-old Aussie who had never sailed before may threaten the viability of their business brand, but, after my fee was safely deposited in their bank account, the polite interaction ended.

No one met us at the airport after our long flight from Miami; in fact, no one there had heard of the Rundletts or their sailing school.

"We've been conned," I muttered as we bumped along the dirt road in a local taxi to the capital, St George's.

Next day, we tracked down Chris and Chrys, who had "forgotten" we were arriving (we had only travelled 20,000 kilometres). Not only that, Chris was too busy to put us through our course, so he had found another skipper: a small, wiry and fiery, weather-ravaged Irishman who we nicknamed Sea Bantam (the builder we had earlier christened Bantam – because he, too, was small and fiery – became Original Bantam).

My concerns deepened on the morning we were due to weigh anchor out of St George's: the Rundletts were seen loading onto the boat cases of rum sprinkled with the odd grapefruit, mango and bunches of green vegetables. It seemed Sea Bantam was an alcoholic vegetarian.

"At least we won't get scurvy," I thought.

Sea Bantam was a ferocious skipper. He drilled us day and night, in between gulps of rum and mouthfuls of broccoli. The Grenadines were beautiful – I celebrated my seventy-first birthday with conch curry on Union Island – but we were usually too tired or sick to fully appreciate the sugar-white beaches and postcard sunsets.

When Sea Bantam ran out of veggies before the next port, he swore, cast a rod over the stern and hauled in some kind of gigantic sea creature, which he wrestled into our rubber dinghy then carved up into steaks while on his hands and knees drowning in blood and scales and guts. He had a life-size human dummy aboard – apart from myself – which he would toss into the sea at some inopportune moment, preferably when we were taking a break after some tough

Sea Bantam was a ferocious skipper. He drilled us day and night, in between gulps of rum and mouthfuls of broccoli.

training manoeuvre, and, with an evil grin, shriek, "Man overboard!" This was his signal for me to rush to the wheel, and tack and gibe and somehow return to the poor lifeless corpse and pull it on board to save it from drowning. I didn't have a clue what to do, but I quickly learned that you had a 50 per cent chance of being right with whichever rope you hauled in. I just hoped for the best and listened for Sea Bantam's "Fucking idiot" to see which way my luck had fallen.

The best was usually bad. I tossed Sea Bantam into the water by taking off too fast in the dinghy; missed the berthing buoys by at least 20 metres every time; dropped the hook to catch the buoys into the water and had to swim after it; and nearly knocked down a wharf when trying to berth against it.

Finally, back in home port, St George's, it was time for our final test. Sea Bantam shook his head.

"You're both bloody useless, and you've got no hope of passing; my reputation is ruined."

"Why don't you go to the yacht club while we're doing our exam," I suggested, pushing US$50 into his gnarled hand for a few rums.

He did. And even though we did our exam straight out of the textbook that we had smuggled onboard, it was still touch and go. We both passed. Just.

Meg and I didn't make Jamaica (not by boat anyway). But we did sail around the Grenadines, St Vincent, the Virgin Islands and the Bahamas.

We were drownings waiting to happen, but we somehow survived.

In the Virgin Islands, I motored around Sir Richard Branson's Necker Island and tried to berth to say "hi" to the Virgin founder. Before we could get anywhere near the attractive-looking beach, a sleek red vessel suddenly launched and a loudspeaker bellowed, "You're trespassing. This is a private island."

I felt like saying, "Tell Richard it's Bob Cheek, and I own Zap Fitness. We've got the same red logo. I'm sure he'd love to meet me." But we left immediately.

The next year we chartered a catamaran and sailed around Tahiti, including Bora Bora, another paradise I'd dreamed of visiting. Bora Bora is the most beautiful island I've ever seen. After that I thought I wouldn't push my luck any further, and I haven't sailed since.

Oh, and the cricket. We knew the Australian coach of the day, Darren "Boof" Lehmann, plus a couple of former Tasmanians, including batting coach Michael Di Venuto and stats man Dene Hills, and we met up with them in Dominica before the first Test. We stayed at the same hotel as the team, and celebrated with the boys as they notched up an easy victory. Boof became a good mate, and he and I would catch up in Hobart when he visited.

Then it was on to Kingston, Jamaica, one of the most dangerous places in the world, where, if you venture into the notorious Trench Town, you're unlikely to return, at least alive. Even Bob Marley was lucky to survive an ambush; and if they attacked Bob Marley, what hope did this Bob have?

One night we ventured out to buy some jerk chicken (you haven't had fowl until you try Jamaican jerk chicken) and wandered down to the Triple Century Bar, owned by legendary Jamaican cricketer Chris Gayle and named after his Test match score of 333. We were sipping on our Red Stripe beers and chatting to the bar manager, when he said, "Chris has just arrived, back from playing one-day cricket in England. Do you want to meet him?"

Did we ever! The 195 centimetre dreadlocked superstar wandered over, bought us a beer, and then said casually, "Hang around until we close, and I'll take you to a street party."

Yeah, right. We hung around but had little hope that the local superstar would keep his word. He did. Chris bundled us into his black Mercedes and was hooning through the back streets of Kingston, nudging 150 kilometres per hour, when the local constabulary, blue lights flashing, flagged us down. An intimidating face pushed through the wound-down window, then squinted, recognised the local hero, and apologised: "Sorry, Chris, didn't realise it was you, man." He proceeded to give him a high five and a virtual police escort to our destination.

You wouldn't have wanted to be here if you weren't with Chris Gayle. Dingy, potholed side street overlooked by dilapidated timber buildings; smoke-filled air; balmy breeze; dozens of sinister looking black men and women in baseball caps and oversize basketball tops with long shorts, all dancing in and out of the gloom to haunting reggae and rap.

As soon as the great man arrived, a group rushed out with a chair, a card table and a bottle of rum. He sat down regally and watched over the scene, as if this was normal practice. Soon he got up and danced, and so did we. The dancers grooved like only black dancers can and the music throbbed in time with my head as the Appleton rum started to turn my body to something like molasses.

I don't remember getting back to the hotel, but I do remember skylarking in the hotel pool with Chris Gayle till about 6am and waking up the other guests. He invited us to his mansion in the hills overlooking the slums of Kingston, offering us breakfast, but by then I'd rummed out.

After that, the tour of England's famous grounds was almost sedate, but satisfying, as the Aussies gave up the Ashes 3–2, and Michael Clarke retired. Steve Smith was my favourite cricketer anyway and would be the new skipper. I'd seen him play his first Test against Pakistan in 2010 and got to know him well in the West Indies.

Eventually my balmy-palm-tree style of business management became frozen English park-bench supervision as I sat among Britain's famous rose gardens, cradling my trusty laptop, and checked numbers and ratios; paid wages, rents, and monthly accounts; and switched money into interest-paying accounts with the flick of a finger on the keyboard.

I marvelled that, on my first trip to England in 1985, my only contact with home – apart from postcards – was a reverse charge call from a red phone box.

About July, I discovered our numbers were slipping. Glancy was overflowing with stress and taking time off work to recover. Much to Meg's horror, I asked her to go back into the depths of a Hobart winter for three weeks to sort out our sales figures while I stayed on in London. Which she did. And flew back to England again.

I arrived home in September after five months away. And Zap was still intact.

Since 2015, I've seen Australia play in just about every overseas Test match, from South Africa to Sri Lanka to New Zealand – part of my ambition to see them perform in every Test-playing nation.

But I doubt there'll ever be another northern summer like 2015. It gave me the satisfaction that, after fifty years in business, I had, in my own small way, finally made it.

Whatever happened next, they couldn't take that away from me.

EATING CROW IN ADELAIDE

Zap was now across two states – Tasmania and Victoria – and my thoughts turned to further expansion to create a national brand. Because we'd decided not to franchise, it was important to develop our gyms in clusters, so an area manager could supervise operations. There was no point in opening one gym in Darwin or Perth or even Brisbane. So we decided South Australia, in particular Adelaide, was the next logical step as Zap blazed across southern Australia.

Typical of the way I operated, I had no sound economic reason. In fact, I'd been warned that Adelaide was a difficult market; and one of our 24-hour competitors, Jetts, had a strong presence there. But, hey, Zap is invincible, right? Who cares about what people think? If we took notice of everyone, we'd never do anything.

I considered Adelaide my lucky city because I'd represented Tassie in football on the Adelaide Oval – as an amateur in 1964 and then in the national Australian Rules carnival in 1969, where I'd carried the flag for Tassie in the opening ceremony and taken on the might of Victoria, South Australia and Western Australia in front of 50,000 fans. How could I go wrong with that rationale? Talk about warped reasoning. And ego. It's amazing what overconfidence can do when things are going well; and how easily you can come unstuck.

My flight touched down in the city of churches on a beautiful summer's day. With unbridled enthusiasm, I hired a car to look around for sites: the hit-or-miss strategy. I'd made contact with a property developer – I'll call him the Crow (South Australians are known as crow-eaters) – and he showed me some potential sites in the city. There weren't any I liked. He thought hard. And, looking back, he probably had a slight tinge of guilt. "I've got this building in Edwardstown which I can show you, if you like, if you've got time..." he trailed off, almost apologetically. It was a warning sign we didn't heed.

Sure, no worries. Edwardstown, where the hell is that? It turned out to be about 6 kilometres south-west of the CBD. The building was untenanted, always a bad sign, but it had good parking and was just across the road from the substantial Castle Plaza shopping centre. And then the clincher...

"I'll do all the fit-out... everything... floor coverings... bathrooms... I'll just throw you the key and you can walk in. Plus, the first three months rent free," the Crow stammered.

I fell for it, again, kidding myself this time it would be different.

Edwardstown's population is only about 5,000 and it already had several gyms, including an Anytime Fitness nearby (again I didn't look around the corner!). And the shopping centre catered mainly to elderly people who had no intention of joining a gym.

Just as we were about to open, Meg fell sick. So, I had to send our northern Tasmanian sales supervisor, Karen, to handle the pre-sell. It was our practice to spend a week in a shopping centre promoting our opening, and we set up in the Castle Plaza, confident we'd make a big

Unfortunately, I was all bluster, not cluster. Edwardstown ensured we never got off the ground in Adelaide.

impression and have prospective members queuing to join, like always. Glancy of the Overflow was there to help set up, but I had to remain in Melbourne, so I kept in touch with Karen by phone each night. I remember calling excitedly the first Monday night after the centre closed.

"How many did we do, Karen?"

"Ah, actually, none, but we had heaps of interest."

Heaps of interest. Danger sign. Tyre kickers, you mean. Tuesday was the same. And Wednesday. And Thursday. And Friday. And the weekend. We didn't sell a single membership in the shopping centre – not one. Meg usually picked up at least 100, and quite often 200. I couldn't believe it and I knew we were in big trouble.

"They're all on walking frames… or picking up pension cheques," Karen lamented as she packed for the long trip back to Launceston.

Zap Edwardstown opened with about sixty members – one of our worst ever – and it never recovered. We got up to about 500, but that was it. Break-even was the best we could strive for. To make matters worse (salt into the wound!) it was aesthetically an unbelievable gym. The Crow, who was actually a good bloke and not to blame for the debacle, had kept his word and done all we had asked. It was 600 square metres of brilliant layout and equipment, all of which remained pristine because, like at Braybrook, no one was using it. It was also hard to get a decent manager, and we ended up flying in most weeks to check on the depressing scene, which took up time and money. To make it worthwhile to pay top dollar for the right person, we needed an Adelaide cluster – and we didn't have one.

Unfortunately, I was all bluster, not cluster. Edwardstown ensured we never got off the ground in Adelaide. It remained our sole gym in South Australia, and a dead dumbbell around our necks. So much for my lucky city – but I had asked for it. Overconfidence and the sense you can't go wrong is a lethal combination.

I returned to Melbourne contrite and determined to become more analytical when selecting sites. Competition was increasing and the hit-or-miss, drive-by, pot-luck strategy had run its race. I hired a Melbourne firm, Spectrum Analysis, to find sites based on demographics and population. They did that all right, but each area now had about five or six 24-hour gyms. Once upon a time, you could move into new markets; now it was about taking members away from other gyms to make a profit.

Times were getting tougher. Much tougher.

WORKOUT 29

FLATTIES
START TO BITE

had a fishing mate, Tommy, an eccentric Vietnam veteran who took his hobby seriously. Whenever he got his first "flattie" (flathead) nibble from our four metre Qintrex out on Tassie's Frederick Henry Bay he solemnly proclaimed, "Mate, I think I've got an inquiry." Much to my mirth.

The fitness industry is the same: along the way you have many competitors nibbling at your business, and you've got to be very careful it's not a fishing expedition to find out how you're doing.

I hadn't set out to sell Zap but when the first nibbles began I felt a sense of relief to know that, after all the hard work, someone out there might actually want our business for a good price, and pride that I had raised my "baby" to this level. Especially after being out on a storm-tossed bay for years, in a leaking boat named Club Silly Wanker, without any bites at all. So I acted pretty casual, but deep down I couldn't wait to find out what they reckoned the business was worth.

Be careful. My first bite came early in Zap's trajectory, less than three years after we opened our first gym, and from an unexpected quarter – the Australian operators of the American franchise Anytime Fitness.

Anytime had started in Minnesota and spread like wildfire across America. I knew two of the three people who had secured the Australian rights to franchise it down under. Richard and Jacinta were both on the infamous roundtable from which I was "sacked", but I considered both of them to be good people, and not part of the conspiracy.

They'd been smart enough to pick up on the 24-hour phenomenon – probably from the round table's Johnny Cash, who was good for something after all – but had taken a different road on the 24-hour journey. I had decided to build my own brand based on the US model; they'd taken the easy way out and bought the master franchise rights for Australia. Because they could hit the ground running, they had jumped out of the blocks faster than Zap but had concentrated first on the vast Sydney market.

Surprisingly, it was Jacinta's brother Justin who made the approach (maybe they didn't want another roundtable). We met at a Hilton Hotel near Crown Casino for the obligatory coffee and circled like two mountain goats about to lock horns – one an upstart young buck, the other battle-hardened and wary.

Justin outlined his reasons for wanting to buy Zap: quick way to expand; heard good things about the business; Anytime hadn't got a strong presence in Tassie (he was right about that, and they never will have, I thought); bullshit, bullshit, bullshit.

Eventually I got sick of the small talk and came to the point.

"I want $12 million if I'm going to sell," I pronounced.

Silence.

"What multiple are we talking about?" Justin countered.

Here we go. If I tell him the multiple of our EBITDA, he'll know what we're making. No chance.

Fitness industry multiples have ranged between two and seven for as long as I've been around. When the British giant Fitness First entered the Aussie market in the 1990s, they were paying seven times for individual clubs. But it was virgin territory, and they could afford to. The consensus was that, if you only have one or a few clubs, two to three times is about it. But if you've built a brand, you can go a lot higher. We'd built a brand – a good one.

The $12 million abruptly wound up the polite conversation. At the time our EBITDA was about $1.5 million – so I was going for eight times. But I didn't want to sell to this Yankee franchising competitor anyway… any time!

We parted with a perfunctory handshake and the usual "I'll get back to you" from Justin. He did, by email, and offered me two-and-a-half times – which he said was the usual price for gyms. I politely thanked him for wasting my time and went back to work.

The next approach was from a messianic, self-termed venture capitalist by the name of Robert Diaz, who appeared to be part of the white-shoe brigade on the Gold Coast – although when I met him on a wet Melbourne day, he at least had the good sense to be shod in tan boots. His firm, Diaz Group Investments, wanted to buy Zap, he informed me in a phone conversation one day. Simple as that.

"How did you get my phone number?"

"It's on your LinkedIn profile," he said.

I didn't have a LinkedIn profile.

Over the mandatory coffee in Collins Street, he regaled me with how Diaz Investments intended to take over the fitness world, and little Zap was to be the launching pad. He then proceeded to rant about how the fitness industry was in deep trouble and had no future, and clubs were lucky to get a two-times multiple these days, and they would all be broke and unsaleable before long.

"If the future's so bleak, why do you want to get into the game?" I tentatively asked.

Robert cut the crap. "Look, I'll be really generous and see if I can

He then proceeded to rant about how the fitness industry was in deep trouble and had no future.

come up to three times because I really like you," he said. The well-worn "like you" line was a bad sign, but worse was when he left the meagre $10 coffee bill in the middle of the table before reluctantly grabbing it.

I was promised the usual email next day. It duly arrived. Robert would give me three times whatever my latest EBITDA was (he hadn't asked for the number) and all I had to do was immediately email him all my financial information, membership numbers, rent agreements, marketing plan and latest tax return. I felt relieved he'd allowed me to keep my family.

I messaged the good Robert and told him what I thought of his offer. His return diatribe told me a lot about the man. It was by far the most abusive email I'd received to that stage. To paraphrase: I was a dickhead who didn't deserve Diaz Investments and he had no intention of dealing with someone who was such a complete moron about gyms with absolutely no idea of their value. Furthermore, he guaranteed the industry was heading for disaster and I wouldn't get two times in a few years, let alone three times. He also knew of another gym chain that was moving to Hobart and would run me out of business. Thanks, Robert.

The next cab off the rank, or should I say Porsche on the starting line, was much more interesting. At least he had credibility. It was Harry from Canberra.

Harry was the son of wealthy Greek property developers who were well regarded in the ACT, and within their portfolio were two large aquatic centres in the national capital. The son and heir had also developed a suite of gyms around Canberra under the banner Lime and Club Group. Our business relationship was brokered by a mutual acquaintance, Paul McClure, who with father Robert owned Melbourne-based equipment distributor Life Fitness.

Harry invited me to Canberra. He picked me up from the airport in his black Porsche SUV and we went to the local golf club for lunch with his Dad (they probably owned it). Later, Harry took me to his gym headquarters, which was awash with staff. Unlike my three-person team, Harry had hundreds, for what seemed like fewer gyms.

Harry was driven and persistent. Together with his accountant and advisers he made several trips to Melbourne for meetings about Zap joining him for an IPO (initial public offering) on the stock market. I was sceptical – especially as Harry wanted to include the property housing the aquatic centres, which, of course, his parents owned. My advisers at Pitcher Partners in Melbourne were also negative on the deal. In the end, I said I didn't want to join the float but would sell the business outright to him for $32 million, which by then equated to about six times EBITDA.

The meetings dragged on. Harry tried every avenue to raise the money to buy us out – but all came to nought. One of the major problems was that our business was more profitable than his. "Who's buying who out?" was the question raised by private equity firms as he desperately sought funding.

During all the negotiations, Harry neatly arranged his papers at the table, flanked by his advisers, and then dipped into his bag and produced a miniature gold Porsche sports car, which he proceeded to stroke often while the talk ebbed and flowed across the room. If the car was full size, it would've equated to hundreds of thousands of dollars. I'm not sure if he wanted a solid-gold Porsche, but the continual caressing certainly provided a welcome distraction from the often-fiery debate raging around the room as we tried to strike a deal.

The caressing continued for nearly twelve months, by which time the little Porsche had lost its gold lustre, and so had the potential deal. There were too many insurmountable hurdles to jump over, and we'd wasted enough time. I pulled the plug and went sailing instead. The Zap team, mesmerised by the gentle polishing of the matchbox-size car, gave Harry the nickname Goldfinger.

To his great credit, Harry eventually dragged in a substantial investor and got a float off the ground as Viva Leisure several years later. By that time, we'd well and truly departed the gym scene. I'm not sure if he's now driving around Canberra in a gold Porsche, but he deserves one for tenacity.

And, Tommy, mate, by this stage I've had plenty of inquiries. I just can't hook that king "flattie"; they've all returned to the depths of the gym floor.

But as you know, mate, like all flatheads, they'll return for another go.

DON'T BE ZAPPED BY YOUR BANK

I guess fossicking for food in Sri Lanka is enough to make any feathered vertebrate cranky, and that's probably why Colombo crows seem to be the world's angriest birds. They're so fierce that five-star hotels pay uniformed staff to go round firing pebbles at them from old-fashioned shanghais (slingshots) to keep them away.

The crow sat on the tiny iron balcony of the dilapidated Colombo City Hotel where I was staying while following Boof and the Aussie cricket team around Sri Lanka. This was no five-star hotel. Despite my arm flapping and yelling, the crow just sat and stared into my face from no more than a metre away – picking out which eyeball looked the juiciest.

Why do I remember? Right at the critical moment, as the Colombo crow readied for attack, my mobile rang. It was my bank – the Commonwealth. And the news was far worse than any crow massacre.

It was September 2016, and the state manager said bluntly, "We can't manually process your member credit cards any more." Those few words immediately cut Zap's bottom-line profit by $2 million and a sequence of events started a downward spiral in Zap's fortunes from which we never fully recovered.

I felt sick. And the crow suddenly seemed like a dove compared with the bank vultures. Let me explain.

As already mentioned, Zap's lifeblood was fortnightly direct debits deducted from member credit cards or bank accounts. It accounted for 95 per cent of our income. Without it we didn't have a business. My holding company, Dockvest Pty Ltd, which owned Zap and Club Silly Wanker (and before that Dockside), was one of the first in Australia to introduce regular fortnightly or monthly direct debits. It revolutionised the previously unstable industry because members could pay progressively, as they worked out, not the full amount up front, and gym owners had predictable cash flows. We did it all in-house, with no outsourcing to third parties. Ever since we started in the 1990s, the CBA had manually processed credit cards that were declined online (for reasons such as past expiry date, changed details, new card). We'd take the details to the bank and they'd access the accounts to pay the amount due. This applied to about 3,500 members each fortnight.

I pleaded for more time, or at least until I got home. To make matters worse my long-time financial controller had resigned over a pay issue while I was away (for maximum effect), so I had nobody in Hobart to reason with the blood-letters. The frustrated crow bade his dinner farewell, and I jumped on a plane for Hobart, ready to confront them.

Frustratingly, Zap was at its peak. For the 2016 financial year our 36 clubs and 30,000 members leveraged a profit of nearly $5 million on the back of $7 million EBITDA. Now we were about to take a 40 per cent hit to the bottom line. To be fair, it wasn't the fault of CBA's Tasmanian state manager, Michael Goss, and his business banking colleagues.

The orders were coming from faceless men in the Sydney head office.

After a flurry of letters and meetings, Gossy (we knew him as Floss for trying to clean us out, which wasn't true but summed up our view of the bank) managed to gain a stay of execution until the end of the year. That at least gave us time to set up a call centre to try to recover the money ourselves – at great expense – member by member. Mission impossible.

We'd recently opened a gym in Melbourne's Surrey Hills that had more space than we needed. So we turned part of the upstairs section into a Zap credit card call centre, employed a team of callers plus supervisor and, without any knowledge of how to run such an operation, picked up the phones. And called. And called.

It was tough going trying to personally contact 3,500 members. Either their phones were busy or they had changed phone numbers. By the time we'd made some inroads, another debit would be run and we were back to where we started – or worse. There were also massive teething problems with technology and staff in the call centre, all of which put added pressure on Dr Strangelove and our fragile, homemade IT system.

By December, we had slightly reduced the number of defaulters, but we desperately needed more time to finesse our system and prepare for the downturn.

I pleaded with the bank for extra time – until 30 June 2017, the end of the financial year – naively attempting to use all my goodwill capital of being a CBA customer for fifty years (which stood for nought in any crunch) and the ability to demonstrate that we were doing our best to reduce the number of declined cards.

Finally, after hours of phone calls, meetings and frustration – where the gulf between the Hobart and Sydney CBA branches seemed as wide as the Pacific Ocean, not Bass Strait, and no one seemed to know what was going on – Gossy informed us that we could have until 30 June.

I'd always had a grudging respect for banks and bankers and was

We were to be executed immediately, no more appeals. And any further protestations would be ignored.

opposed to any Royal Commission into the banking system. It was sobering to learn that they were a morass of mayhem and dysfunction and deserved the scrutiny they eventually got.

We were still on death row, but Dr Strangelove and the IT team set up a staged plan over the ensuing months to handle the 30 June financial hit. Then the bank would abandon us completely, and that included texts to members and re-running the debits every few days for those who didn't have funds in their account. At least we had some order now, instead of panic.

But the bank wasn't happy with that. In late April, Gossy called again and said the bank was being pressured by the credit card companies to end the processing early. Like right now. I told him I expected him to uphold our 30 June agreement. Or didn't the bank have any principles?

Bad mistake questioning those. Of course they didn't. Looking after a good customer? Geez, what were we thinking? Banks wouldn't want people to think they were human.

The message that our lifeblood was being cut off two months earlier than agreed was delivered via email, not personally. We were to be executed immediately, no more appeals. And any further protestations would be ignored.

"Sorry, mate, it was Sydney, not us," Gossy said sympathetically as he flossed our now toothless gums for the last time and explained that head office wouldn't take our calls, or his.

When I broke the news to Dr Strangelove, he collapsed his 195 centimetre frame into the nearest chair and turned an eerie shade of purple, then alabaster, as his body began to drain of all colour so that he looked like a corpse – or, as befitted the Freak Factory, a zombie. And, as far as Zap was concerned, he was, from that day on, a living-but-dead body.

He started to mutter incoherently, "I just can't do it. Can't do it. We're fucked. The business is fucked. We're all fucked." That didn't help my sense of desperation.

Dr Strangelove had done an amazing job cobbling together a homemade software system when he knew nothing about gyms; in fact, the man was a flawed genius. But he had wanted complete control over the system, resisting attempts to share the knowledge with others. As described earlier, he had made himself indispensable. And now that power was destroying him – and us.

Several days later, the inevitable happened. Dr Strangelove resigned. It was a day I'd dreaded for seven years. Our business virtually revolved around what was in his head; he had never written the system code as promised.

We had done everything possible to avoid such a scenario. We put on an assistant, Craig, who was a software developer, not a networker. We had also looked at changing all of our operations to a third party. Apart from the cost of several million dollars for the changeover, the system was set up in such a way that it would take months to reconfigure.

I talked Strangelove into staying until I could find a replacement. And he agreed to write the system code – a mammoth job – before he left. Yet both of us knew that was impossible within the one month's notice he'd given. And so it proved.

Regrettably, Strangelove had a complete breakdown and left work almost immediately, but not before walking around the office muttering that our system was likely to fail at any stage. And so was our business. Which was not tremendous for the already shattered staff morale.

Even to this day, I don't hold any grudges against Strangelove. How could I? He built, in a matter of days, a backyard system, however flawed, that cost the grand sum of $13,000. From that technology acorn grew a business that would be worth millions eight years later. Sure, we had our differences, and we had treated each other with great suspicion, but I doubt anyone else could have done what he did. And he had no idea when he started that his Freak Factory invention would eventually service an empire of thirty-seven gyms.

His replacement, through a recruitment agency, lasted about five weeks.

To add to our financial woes and loss of revenue, we had to refurbish and upgrade at least eight of our clubs at a cost of $3 million plus (cardio equipment lasts only about four years – even less with the amount of human traffic we generated). And Club Silly Wanker was still losing about $250,000 a year – as it had consistently since I started Zap. I had a lot of good friends who had remained loyal members of that ill-fated gym for more than twenty years and I felt an obligation to them. Plus, we owned the building and needed a tenant, if you could call us that. But the time had come to close its loss-making doors.

And, as if that wasn't enough grief, Anytime Fitness, after more than eight years, was finally gaining some traction in Tassie. It had brought in new franchisees and had just opened a club in the city, around the corner from us. Competition was increasing at just the wrong time.

The always sunny Zap outlook had suddenly clouded like the onset of another bleak Tasmanian winter. Even chanting my mantra of "If it was easy everyone would be doing it" didn't work.

And, sorry Dad, at seventy-three years of age I finally wanted to get off my bike, let someone else do the pedalling.

What I didn't know was that, at precisely this moment, another rider was saddling up.

GOLIVER'S TRAVELS

'd known Greg Oliver for decades. We were both considered industry veterans (gym speak for "These bastards have been hanging around forever. Can't they do anything else?") even though he was much younger than me, with fresh, open-faced, matinee-idol looks that made him the son every mother wished she'd had.

We sometimes ran into each other at trade shows and conferences and would stop for a chat – and a laugh about the good old days – but that was about it.

That was what had happened in San Diego in March 2017 at the annual IHRSA conference – months before Zap struck bank troubles – just as we were both entering the auditorium for the opening "rev-'em-up" session by another failed businessperson-turned-motivational-speaker.

Goliver – as I called him, but not to his face – was now CEO of a private equity–backed outfit called Fitness and Lifestyle Group (FLG). They had gobbled up the leading Australian chains Goodlife (of which Goliver had been CEO, when it was part of the publicly listed Ardent Leisure) and Fitness First, as well as the 24-hour franchise operation Jetts. The moves had the normally lacklustre Aussie fitness world buzzing.

"Don't forget Zap when you're chucking around all that money at eight times earnings," I joked.

"Not interested in island colonies," he threw back.

Apparently we were not yet in their sights. Or so I thought.

It was late afternoon on 16 June – I remember the date well – when I received an unexpected phone call from Goliver. After the pleasantries, he got to the point.

"Would you be interested in selling Zap?"

I felt like saying "Bloody hell. With all the shit going on, would I ever!" but managed to be non-committal. We arranged to have lunch the following week.

The venue was the upmarket Sake in Melbourne's Flinders Lane, part of a restaurant stable backed by Quadrant Private Equity, which was also the major fund behind Goliver's FLG. Seated at the table were Goliver, Quadrant partner Jonathan Pearce, and another FLG man named Andrew Pears. Jonathan ordered a sumptuous array of Japanese food, extolled the virtues of Quadrant and FLG, helped despatch an expensive bottle of white wine, and then left me to Goliver and Pears as he excused himself to catch a flight to Sydney.

The rest of the lunch consisted of a discussion on multiples earned by clubs purchased by FLG – who were at pains to point out that media reports on prices handed over for Jetts and Goodlife and Fitness First were wrong – and suggestions I could expect five times if I wanted to sell. Oh, and the kicker: I would have to leave 40 to 50 per cent of the purchase price in the FLG group, to be hopefully restituted later with interest and profit, when the company was sold or floated, which I was told was twelve to eighteen months away. I had no intention of doing this – and walked out thinking at least I had a good lunch, if nothing else.

In reality, I was torn between wanting to keep Zap and the suffering of the past few weeks after the bank pulled the pin. After buying out another shareholder, I now had 75.11 per cent of the company – complete control. My good friend Steve Chopping had the rest and we worked well together. Steve let me run the company unimpeded, but he was always there if I needed him and he gave me great emotional support. In the thirty-odd years I had associated with Steve, I'd never known him not to back my decisions. He deserved a payday as well.

The 2016–17 result was due the next month – and would still look relatively good because the bank hit to the bottom line only kicked in near the end of the financial year. In fact, it was more than good. With thirty-five gyms to our name, profit was more than $6 million; and EBITDA $8.8 million – after taking out the inevitable Club Salamanca loss. So, at five times, the business was worth $44 million. Not bad for eight years' work.

I jumped on a plane to Hawaii the next day for a long-planned short family holiday – more worried about keeping Zap running than about selling it. Goliver called again a few days after I arrived back.

"Look there's no harm in you signing a confidentiality agreement to let us run our ruler over Zap," he said.

I replied: "As long as I can look at FLG as well if you want me to leave money in there." He wasn't too keen on that idea but agreed.

FLG liked what they saw and were keen to move to signing. They couldn't believe how good our margins were; plus the fact that our membership numbers were honest. Most gyms keep non-paying members on their books – suspended members, ones who have departed but may come back – to make their numbers look better. With Zap, I insisted on recording paying members only; it was a true and undiluted figure, which was unheard of in the industry. But, ridiculously as it turned out, I felt guilty about FLG working on a set of numbers that would be hit by the bank bombshell in the next quarter. "Let them find out themselves," said my advisers. I couldn't do that. My morning SOCA time was becoming uncomfortable. I rang Goliver and told him. We agreed to drop the price to $43 million to compensate. At least I felt better.

My resolve was seriously tested by two things: providing all the

Several times I pulled out of the process in protest at what I considered unreasonable requests, but an inner voice kept urging me on.

information needed for the data room as FLG's accountants pulled Zap apart; and trying to manage the chaos in Hobart and keep the numbers up. Several times I pulled out of the process in protest at what I considered unreasonable requests, but an inner voice kept urging me on.

"This is what you've wanted all your life, you idiot," the voice said. "You know the fitness industry is fickle and with this deal you can make more money than you ever dreamed of."

The doubts persisted. We had just increased our prices and it hadn't cost us any members. And the call centre had started to get its act together and make some inroads. We'd also outsourced our computer networking to another company, which showed promise, although it was tenuous.

Meg also hit on a new way of marketing. I noted in my diary in September the reasons not to sell:

Too cheap

Need purpose in life/bored

Nurtured like a baby

Build up to $10m EBITDA next year

IPO, stupid.

And then, at the end of September, I gave in to the doubts. I sought a meeting with Goliver to pull out of the deal.

That was to prove more difficult than I imagined.

WORKOUT 32

MONEY IS NOT EVERYTHING

During this time a quote from the great African–American tennis player of the 1960s and 70s, Arthur Ashe, kept floating into my head: "Success is a journey, not a destination. The doing is often more important than the outcome."

I'd loved my journey with Zap, loved the exhilaration of building a business from scratch and turning a simple name – conjured up in a Mustang convertible as I drove across California – into a quality thirty-seven gym brand. I'd fulfilled my dream of having a Zap "on every street corner"; well, at least in every major town in Tassie. I'd brought fitness and health to the masses and, in just a few short years, had become successful and wealthy. But Arthur Ashe was right: it's climbing the mountain, rather than the view at the top, that is the enjoyable part.

Goliver's phone call had come when I was at a low point with Zap. But now, digital marketing, a streamlined call centre, refurbished clubs and price rises were again driving membership and profit growth in a fitness industry space once shunned by financiers and venture capitalists; now, everyone wanted to be a part of this trendy new world of health and well-being. We were indeed a media company selling fitness. I still had big plans and dreams, and wanted to expand overseas and eventually float the company on the Australian stock exchange; an IPO in our own right.

I was seventy-three but still felt fifty-three. Part of that was due to Zap and part of it to working hard and being around young people with all their foibles and doubts and optimism.

The Hobart *Mercury* had just run a four-page magazine story, with me on the front cover, titled: "Survival of the fittest: How Bob Cheek bounced back". The story started by saying: "It hurt like hell, but former footy star Bob Cheek reckons he's glad he fell flat on his face in politics... lucky really, because he was about to hit the jackpot with a thriving fitness empire." It was like an early epitaph: an exclamation mark on what I had wanted to achieve during the days of despair just eight years earlier. If I could've shuffled down Sandy Bay Road waving that headline, it would have made my life complete.

I'd done it. I'd made it. Time to sell up, I told myself.

But then the story said that I wanted to have fifty gyms within two more years and launch into Asia. And it quoted me as saying, "I figure I've got another 20 years of working so I should have 500 before I retire." And I could, too, you know.

I picked up the phone to Goliver. It was time to pull out of our deal – which I was entitled to do – even though it was October and the mind-numbing sales process had been dragging on for nearly four months. I didn't tell him what I had in mind but I arranged to meet him at a coffee shop over the road from his Melbourne office in the Fitness First gym at Richmond on Friday 13 October at 10am.

"Greg, I don't want to go ahead with the sale. The business has picked up and I realise I love it and don't want to sell," I told him.

He was shocked. "You're crazy not selling for that price in this fickle industry," he remonstrated. "You must have another person interested."

I didn't. I just wanted to keep Zap. Then Goliver started throwing more money about. The price went up and up – and so did the side perks. Rapid-Fire Robert totted up the numbers. The human calculator said this is an offer you can't refuse – for your family and Steve Chopping. Even then, I said I'd think about it.

While driving home, I received another call from Goliver, with even more money if I made the decision now. I said I'd text him an answer before 5pm that day.

I realised the time had come.

After gaining assurances that Zap headquarters would remain in Tasmania; that all staff would be kept in their present positions; and that Meg would have the role of general manager with a salary boost, I texted back to say I accepted the offer. I had dinner with my daughter Melanie, son-in-law Steve and grandkids Olivia and Will at Fish Tank in Brighton and told them the news. Then I went home and cried.

The binding contract was signed in November. Dockvest (formerly Dockside Fitness), the thirty-year-old vehicle I set up to enter the fitness industry in 1987, was sold as the holding company for Zap. Ironically, we kept the building that housed Club Silly Wanker, after FLG agreed to open a new Zap Premium gym on the premises.

I'd had the Wanker for twenty-two years but, unlike Zap, I couldn't wait to wave goodbye to the apartments above; and I'm sure the feeling was mutual. No more complaints about the dropping of dumbbells and the clashing of pin-loaded plates, which one apartment owner once dramatically described as "like the Somme in World War I". No more battles with the banana in pyjamas terrorising the spa bathers. My war was over.

The money, more than I'd ever dreamed of, tumbled into my account on 20 December 2017. Where once I had measured my accounts in tens of dollars it was now millions. But I had no sense of numbers, just of numbness, as I realised the Zap dream was over.

The money tumbled into my account. But I had no sense of numbers, just numbness, as I realised the Zap dream was over.

That night, friends brought champagne to help us celebrate. I tried to be happy and join in the fun with backslaps and "well-dones". Steve Chopping was jubilant. But for me, and Meg, it was a wake. The "baby" was dead.

SHOULD'VE BOUGHT A CHICKEN FROM ROSEBUD

They say once a deed is done, that should be it. Only look back to see if the gate is shut. Let the past bury its dead. And all the other well-meaning aphorisms that don't work.

The day after the sale was finalised I drove to Chadstone Shopping Centre in Melbourne's south-east and went on a mad, crazy, out-of-character spree buying expensive Christmas presents for friends and family: Tiffany's, Mont Blanc, Gucci, Apple... you name it... most of them saw me... and I don't even like shopping. At each store I couldn't help blurting, embarrassingly loudly, "I've just sold my business for millions." Unsurprisingly, the service went to another level.

But when I got home, and looked at the piles of over-priced black-and-white and burgundy bags and parcels, containing a king's ransom in gifts, my only thought was: What the hell have I done? Geez, I didn't even try to beat them down in price like I normally do.

That was my only day of post-Zap sunshine. From then on seller's remorse racked my body daily, like a failed bench press crushing my chest. I wallowed in the what-ifs and regrets and "should've done this and that". I tried to justify it as learning from the past, but really it was a process of agonising over what could have been. I was unhappy, my life had no sense of purpose. There wasn't even any "comfortable anxiety" – and, heaven forbid, I started sleeping in until 7am.

News of the sale leaked and was a big story in Tassie. One TV station put the sale at $70 million, but most reported "more than $50 million". I was sworn to secrecy over the actual figure.

You think your friends and acquaintances will be pleased for you, say that you've done well and achieved much. But most are strangely absent. Maybe they were thinking: "It's one thing that Cheeky's got all these gyms – good on ya mate – but now he's sold for a lot of money, that's different. I liked him better when he wasn't rich."

My wife, Stephanie, and I had coined a phrase more than fifty years ago, for use whenever the inevitable hand wringing about wrong life decisions arose. We were in Melbourne in the 1960s (she came to visit while I was training with Fitzroy) and we hired a car and drove down to the Mornington Peninsula. It was a Sunday and in those days most shops were shut on Sundays. On the way back, we were hungry and saw a charcoal chicken shop open in Rosebud, but we decided we should keep driving until we got closer to the city. Trouble was, we didn't see any more food shops open for business that day – so we went hungry. For the rest of our lives, whenever either of us started to regret a past decision, one or the other would say: "We should've bought a chicken from Rosebud." It usually hit the right spot. Not this time: I could have bought enough chickens from the Zap sale to supply all of the country's KFC stores.

Seller's remorse racked my body daily, like a failed bench press crushing my chest.

But still, regrets of the non-chicken kind tumbled into my mind like unwelcome robo-calls. I realised that I'd been wrong all my life: I thought business was only about making money and being rich, but Arthur Ashe was right: It's the journey that counts. Money is only the measure of what a business is worth. And it's comforting to know someone will buy it for a lot of money. But money's not the end game.

I know I sound ungrateful for my good fortune but, if money is all you're interested in, then it's a sad life. I could now buy virtually anything I wanted: houses, cars, clothes, overseas trips… But for what? You buy a house for $600,000 or $6 million or $60 million. But it's still only a place to live, and, without the right people around you, it's still not a home. And having choices makes you miserable: it's much easier when you don't have all that much, and the choice is made for you; poverty reduces your options. I actually empathised with the mental health problems James Packer suffered by looking after his billions. Even though my net worth was only a fraction of his, it was still the equivalent of billions for me.

I realised Zap had been my life. I realised how much I missed the cut and thrust of the marketplace and building a brand. I was lost. And I was prevented, contractually, from starting anything else in the fitness industry; rightly, the contract precluded me from setting up another like business for many years.

True, the Zap brand is continuing. Initially Goliver wanted to swallow

up Zap into Jetts. But, when he realised Zap was the best-run gym chain in Australia, he changed his mind. In fact, he went the other way, and twenty Jetts gyms in South Australia became part of the Zap stable; so there were now nearly sixty. So what? I'm not there any more.

I went off with Boof and the boys to South Africa to try to forget Zap. I was beside them in Capetown for the notorious sandpaper Test, which tore the heart and soul out of Aussie cricket. I was in the same hotel and saw and experienced the heartbreak and disintegration of men, families and lives. I hugged Boof and said a tearful goodbye after he resigned as coach. He did what he thought was right, even though he had nothing to do with the hare-brained decision to tamper with the ball. The whole scene made me even more depressed. But I realised how one ill-fated decision can change your life forever.

I had always dreamed of buying the perfect waterfront tropical retreat on a white-sand beach. But where? I travelled to Vanuatu and looked at 10 acres of pristine waterfront land with five houses and its own private beach. Previously the only option was a rundown wooden bungalow with hammock; now I could afford the whole lot. But I still couldn't decide.

I remember perching on my Juliet balcony at Port Vila's Grand Hotel, wondering what the hell I was doing. The multi-coloured water taxis scuttled across the blue–green harbour, groaning under the weight of too many Ni-Vanuatu schoolchildren and workers, earning $2 an hour, who were returning to their island homes from the ramshackle collection of buildings that masqueraded as downtown.

Somehow the boats stayed afloat; and the laughter and chatter of the passengers rippled across the water, crashing into my thoughts like a Tsunami of enlightenment. How I envied them, dirt-poor but happy. I was supposedly filthy rich, but miserable.

I was staying in the hotel's most expensive room – the Panorama Suite – for no reason other than because it was the most expensive room. I was becoming lazy, indolent and slothful; drinking far too much duty-free liquor and still trying to comprehend what had happened in the past decade. Maybe, I pondered, I should just go back to Rosebud, buy that roast chicken, cross the highway to the beach, spread a picnic rug and count my blessings. After all, I'm alive, and that's more than I can say about many of the punters I've met along the way.

Fireworks started to shower over Port Vila Harbour in the dusk. It was no Sydney on New Year's Eve but, after three gin-and-tonics, I mused that it must have been like that over the Pacific islands during World War II. It was Port Vila Day. The harbour lit up as the show climaxed. I couldn't help seeing it as a metaphor for my life after politics: darkness and then a display of light and sound that lasted nearly a decade: my Zap life. The journey had been so amazing, I wished it could have gone on forever.

THE COOL-DOWN

My seller's remorse has now turned to seller's rejoice. COVID has smashed into gyms like a cyclone; and although the stimulus-flooded economy is booming again, just as I knew it would, gyms are first in line for shutdowns by over-zealous health officials, playing havoc with their bottom lines. Sad and short-sighted, really, when gyms are the ideal antidote for burgeoning mental health issues and they promote self-esteem and positivity during difficult times. I feel for the industry but I'm glad to be out.

And my throwaway line that I wanted a gym on every street corner in Tassie has seemingly been embraced throughout the country as entrepreneurs, unperturbed by the COVID-induced coma, flood the market with the latest American and Australian franchises and fads. Competition is fierce. Many will fail. But, thankfully, no one is doing POPs any more. It's as though a giant magnet has hovered over the POPs, dragged out every compartment within (minus the pools and spas) – cycling, group classes, high intensity circuits, Pilates, yoga and boxing – and magically turned them into individual boutique studios. I still marvel at the great contradiction of the industry: that little has changed since the Greek era, but it's still possible to lease a cheap room, scatter around some basic equipment, devise a slightly different concept, power it with digital marketing, and sell out for millions. If you follow my rules. And although, post-pandemic, many pundits are flagging the end of bricks-and-mortar gyms, don't believe them! True, COVID-19 isolation ushered in the rise of digital wellness with online gym classes, digital apps, wi-fi bikes and a myriad other tech-driven, on-demand home fitness tools. But home fitness is a lonely occupation; humans are social animals and will always need the interaction and inspiration of PTs and other members. After all, showing off that buffed and ripped body in a gym is much more fun than in a bathroom.

Instead of regret, I now give thanks for my Zap journey – for the luck and timing, for the adventure of a lifetime. It's been hard for me to let go, but Zap is standing up resolutely under the new owners. They finally closed down the loss-making Braybrook gym, but the chain has grown to nearly sixty and I still drive proudly around the streets of Melbourne and Hobart, gaze at my logo shining brightly above the pavements and think aloud, "I started all that." Ironically, after my ill-fated attempt, about twenty Zap gyms are now blossoming in Adelaide, thanks to the rebranding of the Jetts chain in South Australia with the treasured Zap logo. I could've saved myself a lot of trouble all those years ago if I'd known! I haven't set foot in any of the gyms since I sold, just as I haven't been in Hobart's Parliament House since I left politics. The new owners operate them differently from how I did, and I don't always agree. But, hey, it's their prerogative; Zap isn't mine any more.

Now, instead of being perpetually driven to succeed, I appreciate the joy of living. Last year while in Port Douglas I slipped on wet tiles, hit my head and suffered concussion and severe cuts and bruises. I recovered consciousness in an ambulance on the way to hospitals in Mossman and then Cairns. Doctors said I was only centimetres away from more permanent and serious damage to my spinal cord. It made me realise how quickly life can change.

Recently, I went to the fiftieth reunion (actually fifty-first because COVID prevented it the previous year) of the first ever Tasmanian Football League premiership, in 1970, of my old football club, Clarence, played before a record crowd of nearly 25,000 at North Hobart Oval. There I walked among our wounded battalion of knee and hip replacements and listened to cancer scares and spoke with wheelchair-bound friends. Fortunately, I'm still fit and well.

And while money isn't everything, it has given me the financial freedom I've always dreamed of. I can help out my family and friends without ever worrying where the dollars are coming from. And charities and good causes. For the first time in my life I'm giving back to the community.

After I sold Zap, due to the non-compete clause in the sale contract, I looked for other business opportunities unrelated to health and fitness. I wanted to again feel a sense of purpose each morning and to work hard – just as I always had. I invested in some start-ups and joined some boards. But a funny thing happened: I didn't want to work twelve-hour days any more. I still go through my State of Comfortable Anxiety between 3.40 and 4am each day and I usually still get up at 4. But the anxiety isn't as anxious, and the comfortable is, well, even more comfortable. Or should I say satisfied?

I have time for my six beautiful grandchildren: Nellie, Molly, Olivia, William, Otis and the newly arrived Betty (born 11 August). I can travel across the three states where my children, Marcus, Melanie and Lucy, live, to watch the grandkids grow up and play school sport during the day. I have time to decide what's important in my life.

I think more about the people who helped achieve the Zap dream. I used to believe it was all about me; but it wasn't. There was Meg, rising from sales manager to CEO, who shared my vision and overcame incredible personal setbacks to make Zap succeed; and there was the loyalty of unsung heroes like Jess Jarvis on the front desk. Jess, who came to Club Salamanca on work experience and was still there twelve years later; Michelle, who made the ambitious Glenorchy Zap Mega her own and turned it into a powerhouse; Jared, the eccentric personal trainer who became our most loyal lieutenant, willing to go out and unblock toilets at 3am if requested. I thank you all.

And my wife Steph. Zap took its toll on our marriage, and we separated, but we're still good friends. We've been through a lot together. I would not have achieved as much in my adult life without her support. I met her as a wild teenager and we married young and raised an incredible family. She has been the one constant, the stabilising force, throughout my life of football, business and politics; always there, always putting me first, always in the background, never wanting the spotlight; through good times and bad. I can never fully repay her – but now I'll try.

I can also pursue my childhood ambition to write books. My mum always wanted me to be a writer, not a businessman or a politician. Even when I rang her to say I'd been elected Leader of the Opposition in 2002, there were no congratulations. After a long silence she finally said, "That's fine dear, but what about your books?"

Well Mum, now I can write books, purely for enjoyment, and to share my life's experiences in the hope of being able, in some small way, to help others. From entrepreneur to author… Who would've thought?

Maybe books will take me on another magic-carpet ride around the world of literary circles – just like my Zap journey through Gymland. I doubt it, but who knows where life will take you as long as you're still "having a go" – whatever your age or situation.

So, sorry Dad. I'm still firmly on my bike, but freewheeling downhill now. I'm sure you'd understand and be proud of what your simple advice helped me achieve.

Then again, who knows when I'll start pedalling flat out once more. After all, writing is hard work and there are mountains of words to climb.

THE MEMORY ZAPPER

Your one-page workout summary
Read every day to stay business fit

Drawn from more than fifty years in business, sport and politics; and a graduate diploma from the College of Commonsense.

1   You're never too old – it's a mind game.
2   Don't get off your bike – keep pedalling.
3   Be an inquisitive stickybeak.
4   Reach a State of Comfortable Anxiety.
5   If it was easy, everybody would be doing it.
6   Be a benevolent dictator early on.
7   Be an expenses bastard.
8   Work harder, as well as smarter.
9   Be wary of those boasting degrees.
10 Don't employ anyone who wants job security.
11 Don't take government handouts – be your own person.
12 Profit margins are your god.
13 Become a media company that sells your product.
14 Only cowards lose their temper.
15 Avoid business partners if you can.
16 Keep business plans short (one page of dot points).
17 Steer clear of PowerPoint presentations.
18 There's no such thing as work/life balance.
19 Avoid franchises.
20 Suspect everyone and trust no-one but yourself.

THE SUPPORT
TEAM

This may sound strange in light of the early chapters, but I want to thank all the members – well, most of them – at my upmarket gym of twenty-five years, Club Salamanca. True, in my darkest days I christened it Club Silly Wanker, and poked fun at many of the "wankers" to keep my sanity, but the gym spawned some of my greatest friends, who were loyal members from beginning to end. They're the reason I kept it going when the losses mounted alarmingly and I should've slammed shut the doors. If you think you recognise yourself as one of my rather eccentric characters, you're probably wrong. But if any offence is taken, none was meant, and I apologise.

It was those same members, from both Zap and Club Salamanca, as well as family and friends, who urged me to encapsulate four decades of gym life into a business workout model for future entrepreneurs. I hope I've lived up to their expectations.

Writing the book proved much harder than I expected. In fact, my book journey proved to be nearly as eventful and volatile as the wild gym ride. Shortly after starting to write at my home in Melbourne last year, I hurriedly threw some clothes into the boot of my car, said goodbye to my family, and fled northwards to avoid the looming draconian lockdown bestowed on the State of Victoria by Premier Daniel Andrews. A fugitive from COVID injustice.

Most of the first draft was written in seedy motel rooms as I slowly wound my way up the Australian coastline, after clearing the Victorian border and Australia's version of the Berlin wall. Finally, in a rented house at Byron Bay, I tapped out the last words. There was never any doubt what would happen next: I called my good mate Wardy – Mike Ward – a former colleague at *The Mercury* and, in my humble opinion, the best newspaperman and editor in the country. Would he read my book and tell me what he reckoned? He gave it the thumbs up. Maybe mateship played a part in his words of support, but it meant a lot. Thanks, Wardy.

We now had to get a publisher. Again Wardy handballed the book across to another former *Mercury* journo and colleague, Robin Bowerman, now head of corporate affairs with Vanguard Investments, who knew the owner of Hardie Grant, where the manuscript eventually landed.

The *Mercury* connection continued when cartoonist John Farmer, who still draws for the paper under his publishing name Polly, agreed to help liven up some of my chapters with his magical strokes and flourishes. Thanks to all my former workmates. Maybe my time at *The Mercury* wasn't wasted after all.

We were all set to go. But, as I mentioned in the final chapter, *The Cool-Down*, disaster struck. I had finally reached the northernmost point on the fugitive run – Port Douglas – and booked an Airbnb for a week to polish the many rough edges of my work. The next morning, coffee in one hand and phone in the other, I slipped and cracked the back of my skull on lethal rain-soaked outdoor tiles, more like a skating rink than a pathway. I was knocked unconscious and hospitalised. The aftermath was vertigo, dizziness, short-term memory loss and an inability to concentrate for long periods of time. My thoughts mirrored the mental anguish I suffered. Was this a sign from above that I shouldn't publish the book? There was a long hiatus as doubts rose and fell like an overworked lat pulldown machine until, finally, after expert medical treatment in Melbourne, I resumed work with Hardie Grant's editor Sally Moss.

My great admiration goes to Sally, not only for suggesting the title of the book but also for putting up with my prickly impatience, technological incompetence and, at times, ingratitude for her fastidious oversight. You see, when you've been a newspaper editor you think you know everything, and you get upset when changes are suggested to your precious manuscript. Her knowledge of the English language is far superior to mine, and I lost count of the times I was proved to be incorrect. She always acted with grace and good humour and soothed my bruised ego with calm reassurance. Thanks, Sally.

And finally to Courtney Nicholls, publishing director at Hardie Grant, thanks for believing in the book and your continual encouragement to finish what I started.

My gratitude to you all.